MW00654291

THE COUNTIES OF IRELAND

Londonderry

Donegal

Antrim

Tyrone

ULSTER

Down

Fermanagh

Armagh

Sligo

Monaghan

Mayo

Leitrim

Cavan

Louth

Roscommon

Longford

CONNAUGHT

Meath

LEINSTER

Westmeath

Galway

Offaly
(Kings)

Kildare

Dublin

Leix
(Queens)

Wicklow

Clare

Carlow

Kilkenny

Tipperary

Wexford

Limerick

MUNSTER

Waterford

Kerry

Cork

—— PROVINCIAL BOUNDARIES

A Guide to

I·R·I·S·H
PARISH
REGISTERS

Brian Mitchell

GENEALOGICAL PUBLISHING CO., INC.

Baltimore   *1988*

Copyright © 1988 by
Genealogical Publishing Co., Inc.
Baltimore, Maryland
All Rights Reserved
Library of Congress Catalogue Card Number 88-80058
International Standard Book Number 0-8063-1215-7
Made in the United States of America

INTRODUCTION

The Griffith's or Primary Valuation of Ireland and parish registers of baptisms, marriages and burials are perhaps the two most important sources for genealogical research in Ireland. This book attempts to make a search of these records more rewarding for the researcher. By listing the commencement date of all parish registers, it is now possible to identify all churches located in every civil parish in Ireland. As the Griffith's Valuation was compiled on a civil parish basis this means that a researcher using Griffith's Valuation can identify the churches of all denominations and the commencement date of their registers. This book makes the Griffith's Valuation and parish records compatible, as they can both now be identified by the same administrative division—the civil parish.

THE GRIFFITH'S OR PRIMARY VALUATION OF IRELAND

This survey was carried out under the direction of Sir Richard Griffith between 1848 and 1864. It is a record of extreme importance owing to the absence of census records of the nineteenth century for most parishes in Ireland. Remnants of the 1821, 1831, 1841 and 1851 censuses do survive for some parts of counties Antrim, Cavan, Fermanagh and Londonderry. The year 1901, however, is the first year for which a complete census return for all Ireland exists. The Griffith's Valuation, therefore, assumes an importance that it wouldn't otherwise have. It was, furthermore, carried out at a time when the population of Ireland was in sharp decline, with heavy emigration to North America and Australia. The Griffith's Valuation is a comprehensive record in that it lists all property holders, no matter how insignificant the amount of land or size of house they occupied. This survey may, therefore, be the last official record of many who emigrated to the New World.

With the maps accompanying the householders' index to the Griffith's Valuation—compiled by the National Library of Ireland in the 1960s—it is possible to locate all baronies and all civil parishes and their relationship to one another. However, the map reference numbers in the maps accompanying the householders' index don't correspond with the numbers in the *New Genealogical Atlas of Ireland* by Brian Mitchell (Genealogical Publishing Company, 1986). In the Griffith's maps the parishes are numbered in a numerical sequence within baronies, while in the latter civil parishes are numbered in alphabetical order. For example, in the *New Genealogical Atlas* All Saints Parish is number 2 in the County Donegal maps, while it is number 29 in the map accompanying the householders' index.

Each civil parish listed in this book is preceded by the number used in the *New Genealogical Atlas* and followed by the map reference number in the householders' index. This book, therefore, can be used with both the *New Genealogical Atlas* and with the Griffith's Valuation maps.

PARISH REGISTERS

Civil registration of births, deaths and Roman Catholic marriages didn't begin until 1864 in Ireland. Protestant marriages, however, were registered from 1845. Before these dates baptism, marriage and burial details of an ancestor will be found in parish registers. As birth, marriage and death certificates are indexed on an all-Ireland basis, it is probably fair to say that parish registers lose their importance with the introduction of civil registration. For the first half of the nineteenth century and before, parish registers are an indispensable source of information for the genealogist.

The relevance of parish registers to Americans tracing their ancestry is easily demonstrated by the following example. The baptismal records for the Second Garvagh Presbyterian Church begin in 1830. The first page of the register contains the baptismal entries of twenty-one children and the note, "10 of these went to America, 5 dead, 6 in congregation." In other words, nearly one-half of the children baptized emigrated to America. One wonders how many descendants of these ten children born in the small County Londonderry town of Garvagh in 1830 are now living in the States?

At present a major difficulty with the use of church registers is identifying which registers exist for each civil parish and their dates of commencement. The Church of Ireland and Roman Catholic churches have a well-defined parish network which in the case of the Catholic Church does not correspond with either the names or boundaries of the civil parishes. The Church of Ireland parish largely coincides with that of the civil parish and retains the civil parish name. The Presbyterian Church doesn't have a parish structure as such. Congregations generally formed where there was sufficient demand from local Presbyterian families. In those areas with a high Presbyterian population there could be many Presbyterian meeting houses. For example, the civil parish of Ballymore in County Armagh had six Presbyterian congregations by the middle of the nineteenth century. By contrast, in County Wicklow, with fifty-seven civil parishes, there was only one Presbyterian congregation—at Bray. The other Protestant dissenting denominations formed where there were enough like-minded people.

This book locates churches of all denominations, including Roman Catholic parishes, within their civil parish in the middle decades of the nineteenth century and provides the earliest commencement date of their registers.

CHURCH OF IRELAND REGISTERS

The parish structure of the Established Church in Ireland was largely defined in the seventeenth century. Although the Church of Ireland population consisted of only about 12% of the total Irish population, it wasn't until the Irish Church Act of 1869 that it became disestablished. This disestablishment, which took effect on 1 January 1871, was to have serious repercussions for twentieth-century genealogists. The Parochial Records Act now required that Church of Ireland records of baptisms and burials prior to 31 December 1870, and marriages prior to 31 March 1845, should become public records. The parish registers of 1,643 Church of Ireland parishes were thus ordered to be sent to the Public Record Office in Dublin. Luckily, as it turned out, an amendment allowed records to remain in local custody if there was an adequate place of safe-keeping in the parish.

A complete indexed list of Church of Ireland parish registers for all Ireland was printed in the 28th *Report of the Deputy Keeper of the Public Records in Ireland* (1896), giving the baptism, marriage and burial commencement dates for all registers and identifying those records sent to Dublin and those retained in local custody. By 1922 the original records of 1,006 parishes were deposited in the Public Record Office in Dublin while 637 were retained in local custody.

With the fire in the Public Record Office in 1922 all but four of the 1,006 registers were burnt. The loss was offset to some extent by the fact that 637 registers were never deposited in Dublin. Of the original registers burnt, 124 parishes reported that full copies of their registers had been made, while extensive extracts from a number of other registers had been copied. Furthermore, twenty-nine of the earliest registers had been printed before 1922. For example, fifteen registers alone, pre-dating 1700, were published for Dublin city parishes, the earliest being St. John's, with entries commencing in 1619. The effect of the fire was more severe on some counties than on others. In County Dublin, with ninety-nine civil parishes, seventy-two pre-1871 church registers survive of which seventeen have commencement dates between 1619 and 1699, twenty between 1700 and 1799, and thirty-five between 1800 and 1871. In contrast, County Kildare, with 110 civil parishes, has only sixteen registers with pre-1871 commencement dates. Of these sixteen registers, fifteen are records that were preserved in local custody while one, namely Lackagh Parish with an 1830 commencement date, is a transcript of an original record stored and, therefore, lost in Dublin.

In my list I have only listed Church of Ireland registers which contain entries of baptisms, marriages or burials prior to 1 January 1871, as registers commenced subsequent to 31 December 1870 were unaffected by the Act and have all remained in local custody. Furthermore, because of the introduction of civil registration, parish entries after this date are of less value. The absence of a date in my list means there are no surviving Church of Ireland registers, either originals or copies, pre-dating 1871. The date in my list refers to the earliest baptism entry, unless it is stated otherwise.

The commencement date given does not necessarily signify a complete register from that year. For example, the register of Derrynoose Parish, County Armagh, runs from 1710 to 1746 and then restarts in 1822. For the parish of Ardclinis, County Antrim, baptism entries only survive for the years 1831 to 1839. If the

Church of Ireland parish is known by a name other than the civil parish, it is entered against the appropriate civil parish. It is also possible for there to be more than one Church of Ireland church in a civil parish.

With disestablishment many Church of Ireland parishes were no longer viable. This resulted in parishes amalgamating. For example, the parish of Drumgoon in County Cavan now consists of Drumgoon, whose registers commence in 1810, Killesherdiney (1810) and Ashfield (1821). Three registers, therefore, exist for Drumgoon parish.

The list of Church of Ireland registers has been compiled from parish register listings kept in the Public Record Offices in Belfast and Dublin, and from Margaret Dickson Falley's list in Volume I of *Irish and Scotch-Irish Ancestral Research* (1962; repr. Genealogical Publishing Company, 1981). The *Reports of the Deputy Keeper of Public Records in Ireland* were also searched. The 55th *Report* (1928) listed 416 parishes with original registers in local custody. The 56th *Report* (1931) provided a list of transcripts of destroyed registers for 124 parishes. The 28th *Report* (1896) was used to check baptism commencement dates. The ecclesiastical directory of *Thom's Irish Almanac* of 1854 and the *Church of Ireland Directory* of 1987 were consulted to aid in the identification of Church of Ireland parishes.

When using these lists always remember that the church and its parish structure evolved like any other organization. Churches became separated from the old burial places as new churches were constructed. For example, the Old Clondermot Parish Church in County Londonderry was built by the London Company of Goldsmiths in the townland of Clondermot in 1622. Its graveyard contains the tombstone of Colonel Michelburn, governor of the city of Londonderry during the siege of 1689. By the middle of the eighteenth century this church was falling into disrepair, so a new church was erected on its present site in Altnagelvin townland in 1753. By 1867 the Church of Ireland population of the parish had risen to 1,500. A new church called All Saints was, therefore, opened in Clooney townland to accommodate the large number of parishioners living in the Waterside area of the city of Londonderry.

It is very possible for the baptism, marriage and burial records of Protestant dissenters to be within the registers of the Church of Ireland. For centuries the Established Church claimed the right to administer baptism, marriage and burial ceremonies to all Protestants, regardless of denomination, as the exclusive prerogative of the Church of Ireland clergy. In the 1660s, for example, the meetings of Presbyterians, Baptists, Congregationalists and Quakers, as well as Catholics, were broken up and the people fined for non-attendance of the Established Church. In the eighteenth century especially, due to prevailing laws, the records of baptisms, marriages and burials of Protestant dissenters are likely to be found in the parish registers of the Church of Ireland. Until the 1689 Act of Toleration, non-conformist preachers could be fined and imprisoned for conducting services. Until 1782 marriages between dissenters, celebrated by their ministers, were illegal. Until 1844 a marriage between a dissenter and a member of the Established Church was considered illegal if performed by a dissenting minister. Prior to the Burial Act of 1868, which permitted dissenting ministers to conduct burial services, the Church of Ireland clergy held jurisdiction over funeral services for Protestants. Right up to the mid-nineteenth century it is not uncommon to find Presbyterian ministers and Methodist preachers buried in a Church of Ireland cemetery. Clearly, if you have Presbyterian, Methodist, Baptist, Congregational or Quaker ancestry, it is essential that you do not overlook the Church of Ireland registers.

It is also true that members of the Established Church frequently became dissenters. I have a great-grandfather who was baptized and married Church of Ireland but died a Methodist. He apparently fell out with the rector of Drumgoon Parish, County Cavan, and transferred the family's allegiance to the Methodists.

The original registers of the Church of Ireland are held locally, but the Public Record Offices hold transcripts and extracts. The Public Record Office in Belfast holds microfilm copies of most Church of Ireland registers for the six counties of Northern Ireland. The Public Record Office in Dublin holds the transcripts of 124 of the original registers which were destroyed in the fire in 1922.

ROMAN CATHOLIC REGISTERS

The Church of Ireland was able to establish an all-Ireland parish structure because of its privileged position as the Established Church. Owing to its numerical strength, the Roman Catholic Church was also able to set up a parish network which included within it every townland in Ireland. In 1834, 81% of the population of Ireland was Roman Catholic.

The Penal Laws and the active persecution of Catholics resulted in the late erection of chapels in many parishes and the late commencement of many Catholic registers.

In Clondermot Parish, County Londonderry, the first Roman Catholic chapel wasn't constructed until 1791 in the townland of Currynierin. Prior to this, mass was celebrated in the open air "in Ardmore and Fincarn Glen in situations admirably adapted for concealment during the operation of the Penal Law. Fincarn altar is an accidental stone selected by the priest as a convenient substitute for a regular altar. Near the point where a stream, flowing in a deep precipitous ravine, enters the Faughan, and in a picturesque situation within a deep wood stands the Ardmore altar which consists of a wall about 8 feet long with a projecting table of loose stones and two flags forming steps." (*Ordnance Survey Memoirs,* Clondermot Parish, 1834.)

I have largely compiled the list of Roman Catholic parishes from the Catholic parish list compiled by the National Library of Ireland to accompany the county maps in the householders' index to Griffith's Valuation. Where discrepancies appeared I made use of *A Topographical Dictionary of Ireland* by Samuel Lewis (1837; repr. Genealogical Publishing Company, 1984), the ecclesiastical directory in *Thom's Irish Almanac* of 1854 and the *Irish Catholic Directory* of 1987.

The commencement date of Catholic registers was compiled from parish lists kept by the National Library of Ireland. The National Library has microfilm copies of nearly all Catholic registers pre-dating 1880. Access to this microfilm is through Catholic parish listings on a diocesan basis. In my list I have noted those parishes which have no registers pre-dating 1880—Ballycroy, Kilcommon and Moygownagh parishes in County Mayo, for instance. The National Library didn't receive some registers (e.g. Cashel and Rathcline parishes in County Longford). If a Catholic parish has no date against it, it means either no register pre-dating 1880 exists or the register could not be identified in the National Library list. If it is because of the latter reason then the register was probably not copied and is held locally.

Each civil parish in my list has the appropriate Catholic parish or parishes listed against it, together with the earliest baptism or marriage entry. For example, the parish of Kilcolman (Claremorris) in the diocese of Tuam, County Mayo, has the date 1806 against it, because the marriage registers begin in that year, whereas the baptism entries don't begin until 1835.

Catholic registers, especially in the bigger cities, can be of an early date. There are baptism and marriage records for Wexford Town dating back to 1671. Waterford has four parishes whose registers date back to the 1700s, namely, Holy Trinity, with baptism entries from 1729, St. John's, 1759, St. Patrick's, 1731 and Trinity Without, 1797. Dublin City has no less than nine parishes with registers commencing before 1800, the earliest being St. Michan's, which has baptism and marriage registers dating from 1726. Indeed, Dublin City and County are well served by registers with commencement dates in the eighteenth century. From the mid-nineteenth century there was a rapid growth in the establishment of new parishes created out of the older, original parishes. For example, the new parishes of Blackrock in 1850 and Dundrum in 1861 were created out of Booterstown, which has baptism registers dating from 1755. Dalkey in 1861, Cabinteely in 1859 and Monkstown in 1881 were new parishes created out of the original parish of Kingstown, whose registers commence in 1769. I have not included these mid-nineteenth-century additions in the County Dublin list, as in the first instance it will be the earlier, original registers which will be consulted. In contrast, the registers of predominately rural counties often start at a late date. Of the forty-one parishes serving the fifty-two civil parishes of County Donegal, twenty-nine of them have registers that don't commence until after 1850. Nine of the Catholic parishes have registers with commencement dates in the 1840s, while another two have entries from the 1830s. Only one register, Clonleigh, with entries from 1773, goes back into the eighteenth century.

There are a few points to bear in mind when making use of the Catholic parish listing. Firstly, the same Catholic parish can be known by more than one name. This makes for obvious difficulties. For example, the Catholic parish of Couraganeen, on the County Tipperary/Offaly border, and named thus in Thom's ecclesiastical directory of 1854 against Killaloe Diocese, is identified by the name of Bourney and Corbally in the National Library list. The *Irish Catholic Directory* can help overcome this problem as it lists in brackets after a parish the historical name of the parish.

Secondly, it is possible for different parishes in different parts of Ireland to have the same name. For example, there are four Catholic parishes of Donaghmore spread throughout Ireland, namely in Armagh Diocese, County Tyrone, Derry Diocese, County Donegal, Dromore Diocese, County Down and Limerick Diocese, County Limerick. If you are aware of what diocese your ancestor lived in then this should present no problem.

Thirdly, Catholic parishes frequently cross county boundaries. For example, the parish of Castlemore and Kilcolman in the Diocese of Achonry straddles three counties—Mayo, Sligo and Roscommon. A search for an ancestor, therefore, who lived on or close to a county boundary should never stop at the boundary of the county in which he lived.

Finally, when trying to identify the correct parish register to search, one must remember that within the same county it is possible that a civil parish is not contiguous. For example, the civil parish of Ballynakill in County Galway, identified as number 13 in the *New Genealogical Atlas,* is in fact split into four parts, identified as numbers 1, 19, 50 and 105 in the Galway map accompanying the householders' index. It would require the search of six Catholic parishes to cover this one civil parish. The Ballynakill civil parish identified as number 1 in the Griffith's Valuation map, is served by the two Catholic parishes of Kilbride and Ballynakill in the Diocese of Tuam. The Catholic register of Glinsk and Kilbegnet in the Diocese of Elphin, commencing in 1836, covers Ballynakill, number 19, while that part of the civil parish numbered 50, falls within the parish of Moylough and Mountbellew in the Diocese of Tuam. The final part of Ballynakill, number 105, is served by two Catholic parishes, namely Ballynakill and Woodford in the Diocese of Clonfert.

The original registers of all Catholic parishes are held locally. The *Irish Catholic Directory* will identify all Ireland's parishes and the priests serving them.

PRESBYTERIAN REGISTERS

It is very noticeable that the Presbyterian congregations in Ireland are very much associated with the nine counties of the northern province of Ulster.

The Presbyterian Church in Ireland was established in the seventeenth century with the arrival of Presbyterian tenantry from Lowland Scotland who were invited to settle on the estates granted to English and Scottish landlords. For example, in 1613 the parish of Clondermot in County Londonderry was apportioned to the London Company of Goldsmiths, and it soon drew in Scottish settlers, who founded First Glendermot Presbyterian Church in 1654, one of the oldest congregations in Ireland. In County Cavan the town of Bailieborough also dates from the plantation of James I, when the barony of Clonkee was apportioned to four undertakers, all Scotsmen, including one William Bailie. Presbyterian tenantry were welcomed and in 1714 the first minister of First Bailieborough was ordained.

In the first third of the seventeenth century Scottish Presbyterians and English Episcopalians worshipped together. Presbyterian ministers who fled to Ireland to escape religious persecution in Scotland were at first welcomed by the Established Church and appointed to the parish church. Their failure to conform to the practices of the Church of Ireland led to the suppression of Presbyterian worship by 1637. 1660 saw the ejection of sixty-one Presbyterian ministers from the parish churches. Though deprived of their income they continued to minister privately in barns or in the open air.

In spite of continued religious, civil and legal persecution imposed by the Penal Laws and the Test Act, the Presbyterian Church made steady progress. By 1708 there were 130 Presbyterian congregations in Ireland.

One feature of the Presbyterian Church is the concentration of congregations within relatively small areas. Doctrinal differences and disagreement over a choice of a minister often divided the original congregation and led to the creation of a new congregation. In 1733 dissatisfaction with the spiritual condition and doctrine of the main body of the Presbyterian Church within the Synod of Ulster led to the formation of secession congregations which formed themselves into an Associate Presbytery.

A few examples for County Londonderry taken from various congregational histories will demonstrate how dissension within the Presbyterian Church led to the establishment of many new congregations in the eighteenth and nineteenth centuries.

In 1777 a secession congregation was formed at Crossgar by a party which had separated from the congregation of Macosquin. In 1812 some members of Crossgar objected to how the *Regium Donum,* or King's gift, a payment made to Presbyterian ministers, was to be allocated, so they withdrew and formed a new congregation at Ballylintagh. Ballylintagh in turn split to form a secession church at Dromore.

A congregation was established in Limavady in 1696. In 1745, however, a dispute over a successor to minister the Limavady congregation led to the establishment of a new congregation at Drumachose. In 1750 the seceders set up their own church and also called it Drumachose. In 1806 the Reformed Presbyterians built a church in Broadlane.

The small town of Garvagh by 1809 had three Presbyterian congregations. First Garvagh, the original congregation, was formed in 1660. A seceding congregation, later to become known as Second Garvagh, or Main Street, dates from 1771. In 1809 Third Garvagh was formed by those in Second Garvagh dissatisfied over the *Regium Donum* issue.

Presbyterian congregations were established outside the nine-county province of Ulster. Scottish engineers building the pier and extending the railway at Dun Laoghaire, formerly Kingstown, formed a Presbyterian congregation in 1828. When Scottish fishermen first began to come to Howth, County Dublin, in the 1850s, Presbyterian services, in Gaelic, were held on board ship. A mariner's hall was then built. In 1868 a Presbyterian church was built at Killarney, not for a local congregation, but for the large number of summer visitors. Many of these congregations were small. In 1849 the congregation of Summerhill, County Meath, consisted of fourteen families. By 1901 there were only six families attending.

The difficulty presented by this growth of congregations, largely in Ulster, lies in identifying the correct Presbyterian register to search. You will probably find that two or three registers may have to be searched even if you know the exact area your ancestors lived in. My wife, for example, is descended from four generations of Presbyterian farmers from Garvagh, County Londonderry, yet the family's allegiance over the last 150 years has fluctuated between First Garvagh, Second Garvagh and Boveedy Presbyterian churches. Furthermore, some of her Presbyterian ancestors were buried in the original Desertoghill Church of Ireland graveyard. Unfortunately, the pre-1871 Church of Ireland registers for Desertoghill and neighboring Errigal parishes were burnt and no copies exist.

In attempting to identify Presbyterian registers one must remember that the name of a congregation may have changed over time. For example, the congregation in County Tyrone renamed Mountjoy in 1878 was known as Cappagh in the seventeenth century and as Crossroads from 1791. The same name may also be attached to different congregations. The name Drumbanagher, for example, was originally attached to three congregations, namely First Drumbanagher, Tyrone's Ditches, or Drumbanagher, and Jerrettspass, or Second Drumbanagher.

The numbering of the Presbyterian congregations can cause problems, especially with the coming together of the Secession Synod and the Synod of Ulster in 1840 to form the General Assembly. The secession and Reformed Presbyterian churches in my list refer to those congregations that didn't join the union in 1840.

The numbering in my list is that applicable after 1840. For example, West Church in Ballymena, County Antrim, was known as Second Ballymena when it set up in 1828, but it became Third when High Kirk, the original seceding congregation, joined the General Assembly as Second Ballymena.

The list of Presbyterian congregations has been compiled from the ecclesiastical directory in *Thom's Irish Almanac* of 1854, the *Presbyterian Church in Ireland Directory* of 1986 and *A History of Congregations in the Presbyterian Church in Ireland, 1610–1982* by the Presbyterian Historical Society of Ireland (Belfast, 1982). The commencement date of the Presbyterian registers was compiled from the list of parish registers kept in the Public Record Office in Belfast and from the list compiled by Margaret Dickson Falley in *Irish and Scotch-Irish Ancestral Research*. The date in my list, in nearly all cases, refers to the earliest baptism entry.

In the twentieth century many congregations have amalgamated into bigger and more viable ones. For example, the five County Donegal congregations of Carrigart & Creeslough, Milford, Fannet, Dunfanaghy and Rathmullan are now united. In County Monaghan, population decline resulted, in 1972, with the congregations of Cahans and Derryvalley uniting with First Ballybay. This means united congregations will have more than one register. In my list some united congregations have only one date against them, i.e. the earliest register. For example, in County Tyrone First and Second Newtownstewart united in 1903 and the earliest register dates back to 1848. However, there should be two registers to 1903 for this united congregation.

Presbyterian registers are still held locally but the Public Record Office in Belfast holds microfilm copies of many of them, especially for the six counties in Northern Ireland.

OTHER PROTESTANT DISSENTING RECORDS

Methodists

The Methodists did not begin to develop their own churches until after 1816. Before that date the Methodist movement did attract large numbers of Presbyterians and Church of Ireland members who formed local Methodist societies, but their baptism, marriage and burial records continued to be entered in the registers of their parent church.

In 1821, for example, it was reported that the Presbyterian congregation of Rahugh in County Westmeath "since Mr Harpur's death (i.e. the former Presbyterian minister) the church and congregation in Rahue, being left in a deserted state, these Presbyterians had become Methodists." Owing to the small size of their congregations, many Methodists wouldn't have had a purpose-built building for worship. In Maghera parish, for example, in County Londonderry, a Methodist preacher held a meeting once a month in 1836 in the house of William Henry which was attended by twelve members.

From 1816 Wesleyan Methodists allowed their preachers to administer the sacraments of baptism and holy communion. The Primitive Wesleyan Methodists, however, would not allow their preachers to administer the sacraments, so their records will still be found in Church of Ireland and Presbyterian registers.

No attempt is made in my list to distinguish between the Primitive Wesleyan and Wesleyan Methodists, who united in 1878. The ecclesiastical directory of *Thom's Irish Almanac* will identify Methodist churches. Methodist registers are held locally. All dates showing the commencement of Methodist registers were obtained from the parish list in the Public Record Office in Belfast.

Baptists and Congregationalists

Baptists and Congregationalists first came to Ireland in great numbers during the period of the Commonwealth. They constituted a large part of Cromwell's army in Ireland from 1649 to 1655. From 1655 many of them were assigned forfeited lands as payment for their army service. Many, however, sold their land and emigrated.

As with the Methodists, records of their baptisms, marriages and burials are more likely to be found within the parish registers of the Church of Ireland. Due to their small numbers and their isolation, many of those who did remain in Ireland became members of the Established Church.

The ecclesiastical directory of *Thom's Irish Almanac* will identify the Baptist and Congregationalist congregations. Their registers are held locally. All dates for the commencement of their registers were obtained from the parish list in the Public Record Office in Belfast.

Quakers

The first Quaker meeting was established in Ireland in 1654 at Lurgan, County Armagh. As Quakers attached great value to the keeping of birth, marriage and death records, and as most Quaker meetings were established in the one hundred years from 1654, it means many comprehensive records of an early date survive.

Many meetings were merely set up in a member's house. For example, when Robert Sandhams became a Quaker in 1655 he held a Quaker meeting in his house in Youghal, County Cork, until a meeting house was built in 1681.

Owing to the quality of their records, I have in my list attempted to identify the locations of all Quaker meetings, even those that didn't survive into the nineteenth century. In 1711, for example, a meeting was settled at Charleville, County Cork. A meeting house was built but it was closed by 1740. Many Quaker meetings failed owing to their small size.

I used the section on Quaker records in *Irish and Scotch-Irish Ancestral Research* to compile the Quaker list. The Public Record Office in Belfast holds all Quaker records for the province of Ulster. The Society of Friends in Dublin holds the Quaker records for southern Ireland.

Brian Mitchell

Acknowledgements

Many thanks to Deidre McCauley and Hilary Roulston of the typing pool of the North West Centre for Learning and Development (Londonderry, Northern Ireland) who did a marvelous job in typing and proofreading the final draft of the manuscript.

KEY

The sequence followed in this book for each civil parish is as follows:

1. The number preceding the civil parish represents the map reference number used in the *New Genealogical Atlas of Ireland.*

2. The name of the civil parish in alphabetical order within county.

3. The number following the civil parish represents the reference number used in the county maps accompanying the householders' index to the Griffith's Valuation.

4. Church of Ireland Parish.
   a) If no name is given then the Church of Ireland parish is known by the civil parish name.
   b) A name is only listed when a Church of Ireland church or parish is known by a name other than the civil parish name.
   c) The date represents the earliest commencement date of baptism registers, except where stated otherwise.
   d) If there is no date against the civil parish name, then no pre-1871 Church of Ireland register survives.

5. Roman Catholic Parish.
   a) The name or names of the Roman Catholic parish or parishes serving that civil parish are given.
   b) The date represents the earliest baptism or marriage entry in the Catholic register.
   c) No date means the Catholic parish couldn't be identified in the National Library list. A register, however, should be held locally.

6. Presbyterian Congregation.
   a) The name or names of Presbyterian congregations located within the civil parish are given.
   b) The date represents, in almost every case, the earliest baptism register existing for that congregation.
   c) The names of those congregations that united or were dissolved, and the year in which it occurred, are given in brackets.

7. Other Protestant dissenting congregations.
   For these denominations the dates of the earliest baptism registers are given when they could be identified.
   The symbols used are as follows:
   R.P. = Reformed Presbyterian Congregation
   S.P. = Secession Presbyterian Congregation
   M.   = Methodist Congregation
   C.   = Congregationalist Congregation
   B.   = Baptist Congregation
   Q.   = Quaker Meeting
   Unlike the other denominations the presence of a name doesn't mean the Quaker meeting was still operational by the mid-nineteenth century. It merely means a Quaker meeting was at one time established in this civil parish.

NGA No.	CIVIL PARISH	GV No.	CHURCH OF IRELAND	ROMAN CATHOLIC	PRESBYTERIAN	OTHERS
1	Aghagallon	80		Aghagallon & Ballinderry 1828		
2	Aghalee	81	1782	Aghagallon & Ballinderry 1828		
3	Ahoghill	29, 30	1811	Ahoghill 1833	Ahoghill – 1st 1841 2nd or Trinity 1835 3rd or Brookside 1859	
4	Antrim	48	1700	Antrim 1874	Antrim – 1st 1670 Millrow 1726 High Street 1850	M. Antrim 1829 Q. Antrim
5	Ardclinis	18	1831	Carnlough 1869		
6	Armoy	6	1854	Armoy 1848	Armoy 1842	
7	Ballinderry	79	1805	Aghagallon & Ballinderry 1828	Ballinderry	Q. Ballinderry
8	Ballintoy	2	1845 marriages only	Ballintoy 1872	Toberkeigh 1830 Croaghmore (united with Toberdoney 1957)	
9	Ballyclug	33	1841	Braid & Glenravel 1825		
10	Ballycor	47	or Ballyeaston 1866	Ballyclare 1869	Ballyeaston – 1st 1814 2nd 1826	
11	Ballylinny	59, 61		Ballyclare 1869	Ballylinny 1837	C. Ballycraigy
12	Ballymartin	70		Antrim 1874 Ballyclare 1869		
13	Ballymoney	12	1807	Ballymoney & Derrykeighan 1853	Ballymoney – 1st 1751 2nd or Trinity 1845 3rd or St. James' 1825 Roseyards 1845 Drumreagh 1864 Garryduff	B. Ballymoney Q. Ballynacree
14	Ballynure	57	1812	Ballyclare 1869	Ballynure 1819	M. Ballynure 1843 C. Straid 1837
15	Ballyrashane	10		Portrush & Bushmills 1844	Ballyrashane 1863 Ballywatt 1867	

1

NGA No.	CIVIL PARISH	GV No.	CHURCH OF IRELAND	ROMAN CATHOLIC	PRESBYTERIAN	OTHERS
16	Ballyscullion	40		Duneane 1834		
17	Ballywillin	7	1826	Portrush & Bushmills 1844	Portrush 1843 Ballywillin 1840	
18	Belfast	74	Christ Church 1835 Mariner's Chapel 1868 St. Anne's, Shankill 1745 St. George 1817 St. John, Malone 1839 St. Mark, Ballysillan 1856 St. Mary's 1867 St. Marys Magdalene 1847 St. Matthews 1846 St. Stephens 1868 Trinity 1844 Upper Falls 1855	Greencastle 1854 Holycross 1868 St. Joseph's 1872 St. Malachy's 1858 St. Mary's 1867 St. Patrick's 1798 St. Peter's 1866	Agnes Street 1868 Albert Street 1852 Argyle Place 1853 Ballysillan 1839 Belmont 1862 Berry Street 1861 College Square North 1845 College Street South 1863 Crescent 1831 Donegal Street 1824 Cliftonville 1825 Duncairn 1861 Ekenhead 1864 Eglinton 1840 Fisherwick 1810 Fitzroy 1820 Great Victoria Street 1860 Malone 1837 May Street 1835 Rosemary Street 1723 St. Enoch's 1853 Sinclair Seamen's 1854 Townsend Street 1835 York Street 1840	S.P. 1st Non Subscribing 1757 M. Agnes Street 1864 M. Carlisle Memorial 1877 M. Crumlin Road 1878 M. Donegal Square 1815 M. Frederick Street 1841 M. Hydepark 1834 M. Jennymount 1873 M. Knock 1874 M. Ligoniel 1870 M. Newtownards Road 1864 M. Ormeau Road 1870 M. Salem New Connection 1829 M. Shankill Road 1874 M. University Road 1865 C. Belfast B. Belfast
19	Billy	9	Dunseverick 1832	Ballintoy 1872 Portrush & Bushmills 1844	Toberdoney	
20	Blaris	84	or Lisburn 1639 Christ Church 1849	Blaris (Lisburn) 1840	Lisburn – 1st 1692 Railway Street 1860 Sloan Street 1861 Maze 1856	M. Lisburn 1827 M. Broomhedge or Priesthill 1837 Q. Lisburn Q. Lisnagarvy
21	Camlin	75		Glenavy & Killead 1848		S.P. Crumlin 1839
22	Carncastle	36		Larne 1821 Tickmacrevan (Glenarm) 1825		S.P. Carncastle 1832

COUNTY ANTRIM

NGA No.	CIVIL PARISH	GV No.	CHURCH OF IRELAND	ROMAN CATHOLIC	PRESBYTERIAN	OTHERS
23	Carnmoney	65	1788 Whitehouse 1840 Jordanstown 1868	Greencastle 1854	Carnmoney 1708 Whiteabbey	C. Carnmoney
24	Carrickfergus	66	1740	Carrickfergus 1821	Carrickfergus – 1st 1823 2nd or Joymount 1852 Woodburn 1819	R.P. Loughmorne 1848 S.P. Carrick-fergus M. Carrick-fergus 1826 C. Carrick-fergus 1819 B. Carrick-fergus 1864
25	Connor	35		Braid & Glen-ravel 1825	Connor 1819 Kells 1874	S.P. Kells-water
26	Craigs	27	1839	Rasharkin 1848	Cullybackey 1812	R.P. Cully-backey M. Cullybackey 1839
27	Cranfield	45		Duneane 1834		
28	Culfeightrin	4	1805 burials	Culfeightrin 1825 Cushendun 1848		
29	Derryaghy	78	1696 Stoneyford 1845	Derryaghy 1877		
30	Derrykeighan	11		Ballymoney & Derrykeighan 1853	Dervock 1827 Benvarden 1864	
31	Donegore	49		Antrim 1874	Donegore – 1st 1806 2nd 1845	
32	Drumbeg	73A		Derryaghy 1877	Dunmurry 1860	
33	Drummaul	42	1823	Randalstown 1825	Randalstown – 1st 1837 2nd 1838 Old Con-gregation 1853	S.P. Craigmore
34	Dunaghy	25		Dunloy (Cloughmills) 1860	Clough 1855 Killymurris	R.P. Clough-mills
35	Duneane	44		Duneane 1834	Duneane	
36	Dunluce	8	1809	Ballymoney & Derrykeighan 1853 Portrush & Bushmills 1844	Dunluce 1865 Bushmills 1820	
37	Finvoy	20	1811	Rasharkin 1848	Finvoy 1843 Dunloy 1845	
38	Glenavy	77	1707	Glenavy & Killead 1848		M. Glenavy 1879

3

NGA No.	CIVIL PARISH	GV No.	CHURCH OF IRELAND	ROMAN CATHOLIC	PRESBYTERIAN	OTHERS
39	Glenwhirry	34		Braid & Glen-ravel 1825	Glenwhirry 1845	
40	Glynn	56	1838	Larne 1821		
41	Grange of Bally-scullion	41		Duneane 1834	Grange 1824	B. Grange
42	Grange of Doagh	51		Ballyclare 1869	Ballyclare 1857	M. Ballyclare 1843
43	Grange of Drum-tullagh	5		Ballintoy 1872	Mosside 1842	
44	Grange of Dundermot	24		Dunloy (Clough-mills) 1860		
45	Grange of Inis-pollen	16		Cushendun 1848		
46	Grange of Killy-glen	38		Larne 1821		
47	Grange of Layd	15		Cushendun 1848		
48	Grange of Muckamore	67	Muckamore 1847	Antrim 1874	Muckamore 1846	Q. Grange
49	Grange of Nilteen	52		Antrim 1874		
50	Grange of Shil-vodan	43		Braid & Glen-ravel 1825		R.P. Eskylane 1874
51	Inver	54	Inver & Larne 1806	Larne 1821		
52	Island Magee	53		Larne 1821	Island Magee – 1st 1829 2nd	
53	Kilbride	50		Antrim 1874	Kilbride	
54	Killagan	21		Dunloy (Clough-mills) 1860		
55	Killead	68, 69		Glenavy & Killead 1848	Killead 1826	S.P. Loanends
56	Kilraghts	13		Ballymoney & Derrykeighan 1853	Kilraghts – 1st 1836 2nd 1858	
57	Kilroot	60	Kilroot & Templecorran 1848	Carrickfergus 1821		
58	Kilwaughter	37		Larne 1821		
59	Kirkinriola	28, 30	or Ballymena 1789	Kirkinriola 1847	Ballymena – 1st 1824 2nd or High Kirk 1837 3rd or West Church 1829 4th or Welling-ton Street 1863 Cloughwater 1852	S.P. Ballymena 1849 M. Ballymena 1879 B. Ballymena 1865

NGA No.	CIVIL PARISH	GV No.	CHURCH OF IRELAND	ROMAN CATHOLIC	PRESBYTERIAN	OTHERS
60	Lambeg	73	1810	Derryaghy 1877		
61	Larne	39	1806	Larne 1821	Larne – 1st 1826 2nd or Gardenmore	M. Larne 1878 C. Larne
62	Layd	17	1826	Cushendall 1837 Cushendun 1848	Cushendall 1853	
63	Loughguile	14		Loughguile 1845	Ballyweaney 1862	
64	Magheragall	82	1772	Blaris (Lisburn) 1840	Magheragall 1845	M. Magheragall 1827
65	Magheramesk	83		Aghagallon & Ballinderry 1828		
66	Newton Crommlin	22	1831	Rasharkin 1848	Newtown Crommlin 1835	
67	Portglenone	26		Portglenone 1864	Portglenone – 1st 1814 2nd 1821 (dissolved 1910) 3rd	
68	Racavan	32	Racavan & Skerry 1805	Braid & Glenraval 1825	Broughshane – 1st 1830 2nd 1868 Buckna 1828	B. Broughshane
69	Raloo	55		Larne 1821	Raloo 1840	S.P. Raloo 1859
70	Ramoan	3		Ramoan (Ballycastle) 1838	Ballycastle 1829	
71	Rasharkin	23		Rasharkin 1848	Rasharkin 1834	
72	Rashee	46		Ballyclare 1869		
73	Rathlin	1	1845	Ramoan (Ballycastle) 1838		
74	Shankill	72	See Belfast	See Belfast	See Belfast	See Belfast
75	Skerry	31	1805	Braid & Glenraval 1825		
76	Templecorran	58	1848	Larne 1821		S.P. Ballycarry 1832
77	Templepatrick	56, 62, 63, 64, 71	1827	Antrim 1874 Ballyclare 1869 Greencastle 1854	Templepatrick 1758 Lylehill 1832	S.P. Templepatrick 1796 M. Mallusk 1843
78	Tickmacrevan	19	1718	Tickmacrevan (Glenarm) 1825 Carnlough 1869	Glenarm 1850 Carnal Banagh 1862	S.P. Glenarm
79	Tullyrusk	76		Glenavy & Killead 1848	Dundrod 1829	

NGA No.	CIVIL PARISH	GV No.	CHURCH OF IRELAND	ROMAN CATHOLIC	PRESBYTERIAN	OTHERS
1	Armagh	14	1750	Armagh 1796	Armagh – 1st 1707 2nd 1825 3rd or the Mall 1837 (2nd & 3rd united 1916)	M. Armagh 1815 C. Armagh
2	Ballymore	21	1783	Ballymore & Mullaghbrack 1843	Clare 1838 Tandragee 1835 1st Drum – banagher 1832 Cremore 1831 Poyntzpass 1850 Tyrone's Ditches 1854	M. Tandragee 1836 B. Tandragee 1872
3	Ballymyre	23	Ballymoyer 1820	Loughgilly 1825		
4	Clonfeacle	3		Clonfeacle 1814		
5	Creggan	25	1808	Creggan Lower 1845 Creggan Upper 1796	Creggan 1835	
6	Derrynoose	15	1710	Derrynoose 1835		
7	Drumcree	5	1780 Portadown 1826 St. Saviour, Portadown 1858	Drumcree 1844	Portadown – 1st 1822 2nd 1868	M. Portadown 1830
8	Eglish	11	1803	Eglish 1862	Knappagh 1842	M.Killymaddy 1815
9	Forkill	28		Forkhill 1844		
10	Grange	13	1780	Armagh 1796		
11	Jonesborough	29	1812	Faughart 1851		
12	Keady	16	1780	Derrynoose 1835	Keady – 1st 1815 2nd 1819 Tassagh 1843	
13	Kilclooney	20	1832	Ballymacnab 1844	Cladymore 1848	R.P. Ballylane
14	Kildarton	17		Armagh 1896		
15	Killevy or Mullaghglass	26	Camlough 1832 Drumbanagher 1838	Killeavy Lower 1835 Killeavy Upper 1832 Dromintee 1853	Bessbrook 1854	M. Bessbrook 1830
16	Killyman	2		Drumglass, Killyman and Tullyniskin 1821		
17	Kilmore	6	1789 Mullavilly 1821	Kilmore 1845	Ahorey 1838 Richhill 1848	M. Kilmore 1815 M. Richhill 1815 C. Richhill Q. Ballyhagen Q. Richhill

COUNTY ARMAGH

NGA No.	CIVIL PARISH	GV No.	CHURCH OF IRELAND	ROMAN CATHOLIC	PRESBYTERIAN	OTHERS
18	Lisnadill	19	Aghavilly 1844	Ballymacnab 1844	Armaghbrague 1870	
19	Loughgall	4	1706 Annaghmore 1856	Loughgall 1833	Loughgall 1842 Vinecash 1838	M. Loughgall 1815 M. Derrylee 1874 M. Charlemont Q. Charlemont
20	Loughgilly	22	1804	Loughgilly 1825	Mount Norris 1833 Tullyallen 1795 Kingsmills 1842	R.P. Ballenan 1860
21	Magheralin	10		Magheralin 1815		
22	Montiaghs	7	or Ardmore 1822	Seagoe 1836	Bellville 1863	M. Bannfoot 1823
23	Mullaghbrack	18	1737	Ballymore & Mullaghbrack 1843	Markethill – 1st 1843 2nd 1821 (united 1919) Drumminis 1859 Redrock (united with Drumminis 1923)	M. Markethill 1830
24	Newry	27	1807	Newry 1818	Newry – 1st or Sandys Street 1829 2nd or Downshire Road 1849 3rd or Riverside 1863 (dissolved 1883)	R.P. Newry M. Newry 1830 C. Newry
25	Newtownhamilton	24	1823	Creggan Lower 1845	2nd Newtown-hamilton 1823 Clarkesbridge 1833 (united with 1st New-townhamilton 1887)	S.P. Tully-vallen
26	Seagoe	8	1672	Seagoe 1836	Portadown – 1st 1822 2nd 1868	
27	Shankill	9	1681	Shankill 1822	Lurgan – 1st 1746 Hill Street 1861	M. Lurgan 1823 Q. Lurgan
28	Tartaraghan	1	1824 Milltown 1840	Loughgall 1833	Tartaraghan 1849	M. Cranagill 1871
29	Tynan	12	1686 Killylea 1845	Tynan 1822	Lislooney 1836 Middletown 1829 Drumhillery 1829	M. Killylea 1815

7

NGA No.	CIVIL PARISH	GV No.	CHURCH OF IRELAND	ROMAN CATHOLIC	PRESBYTERIAN	OTHERS
1	Agha	32		Bagenalstown 1820 Leighlinbridge 1783		
2	Aghade	43	1740	Ballon 1782		
3	Ardoyne	23		Ballon 1782		
4	Ardristan	25		Tullow 1763		
5	Ballinacarrig	6		Tinryland 1813		
6	Ballon	42		Ballon 1782		
7	Ballycrogue	7		Tinryland 1813		
8	Ballyellin	36		Bagenalstown 1820 Ballon 1782 Borris 1782		
9	Baltinglass	13		Rathvilley 1797		
10	Barragh	45	1831	Clonegall 1833		
11	Carlow	4	1744	Carlow 1769	Carlow 1820 (united with Athy 1936)	M. Carlow Q. Carlow
12	Clonmelsh	5		Carlow 1769 Leighlinbridge 1783		
13	Clonmore	22	1845 marriages	Clonmore 1813		
14	Clonygoose	37		Borris 1782		
15	Cloydagh	26		Leighlinbridge 1783		
16	Crecrin	21		Clonmore 1813		
17	Dunleckny	33	1791	Bagenalstown 1820		
18	Fennagh	24	1796 Tullow 1696	Ballon 1782 Myshall 1822 Tullow 1763		
19	Gilbertstown	40		Ballon 1782		
20	Grangeford	9		Tullow 1763		
21	Hacketstown	19	1845 marriages	Hacketstown 1820		
22	Haroldstown	18		Hacketstown 1820		
23	Kellistown	8		Ballon 1782		
24	Killerrig	3		Tullow 1763		
25	Killinane	30		Leighlinbridge 1783		
26	Kiltegan	15		Hacketstown 1820		

NGA No.	CIVIL PARISH	GV No.	CHURCH OF IRELAND	ROMAN CATHOLIC	PRESBYTERIAN	OTHERS
27	Kiltennell	38	1837	Borris 1782		
28	Kineagh	12		Rathvilley 1797		
29	Lorum	35		Bagenalstown 1820		
30	Moyacomb	46	or Clonegal 1792	Clonegall 1833		
31	Myshall	44	1814	Myshall 1822		
32	Nurney	31		Bagenalstown 1820		
33	Oldleighlin	28	1781	Leighlinbridge 1783		
34	Painestown	1	& St. Anne's 1833	Carlow 1769		
35	Rahill	11		Rathvilley 1797		
36	Rathmore	17		Rathvilley 1797		
37	Rathvilly	14	1826	Rathvilley 1797		
38	St. Mullin's	47		St. Mullin's 1796 Borris 1782		
39	Sliguff	34		Bagenalstown 1820 Borris 1782		
40	Straboe	16		Rathvilley 1797		
41	Templepeter	41		Ballon 1782		
42	Tullowcreen	27		Leighlinbridge 1783		
43	Tullowmagimma	10		Tinryland 1813		
44	Tullowphelim	20	Aghold 1700	Tullow 1763		
45	Ullard	39		Graiguenamanagh 1818		
46	Urglin	2	(Rutland Church) 1710	Ballon 1782 Tullow 1763 Tinryland 1813		
47	Wells	29		Leighlinbridge 1783		

COUNTY CAVAN

NGA No.	CIVIL PARISH	GV No.	CHURCH OF IRELAND	ROMAN CATHOLIC	PRESBYTERIAN	OTHERS
1	Annagelliff	13	1804	Urney & Annagelliffe 1812		
2	Annagh	16	or Belturbet 1801 Killoughter 1827 St. John (Cloverhill) 1861	Anna East 1845 Anna West 1849 Annagh 1864	Belturbet	Q. Belturbet
3	Bailieborough	23	1744	Killann 1835	Bailieborough – 1st or Corglass 1845 2nd or Trinity 1863 Seafin 1871	M. Bailie-borough
4	Ballintemple	26		Ballintemple 1862		
5	Ballymachugh	28	1816	Drumlumman South & Bally-machugh 1837		
6	Castlerahan	32		Castlerahan & Munterconnaught 1751	Ballyjamesduff 1845 (united with Bellasis 1980)	M. Ballyjames-duff
7	Castleterra	11	1800	Castleterra 1763		Q. Ballyhaise
8	Crosserlough	30	or Kildrumferton 1801	Crosserlough 1843		
9	Denn	14		Denn 1856		
10	Drumgoon	19	1802	Drumgoon 1829	Cootehill – 1st 1870 2nd 1822 (united 1870)	M. Cootehill Q. Cootehill
11	Drumlane	6	Quivy 1854	Drumlane 1836		
12	Drumlumman	27		Drumlumman North 1859 Drumlumman South & Ballymachugh 1837		
13	Drumreilly	4		Drumreilly 1867		
14	Drung	17	1785	Drung		
15	Enniskeen	24		Kingscourt 1838	Ervey	
16	Kilbride	29		Kilbride (Mount Nugent) 1832		
17	Kildallan	7	1856	Kildallan & Tomregan 1867		
18	Kildrumsherdan	18	or Killesher-diney 1810 Ashfield 1821	Kilsherdany 1803	Kilmount 1866	

10

NGA No.	CIVIL PARISH	GV No.	CHURCH OF IRELAND	ROMAN CATHOLIC	PRESBYTERIAN	OTHERS
19	Killashandra	8	1735	Killeshandra 1835	Killashandra 1743	
20	Killinagh	1		Killinagh 1869		
21	Killinkere	31	Billis 1840	Killinkere 1766	Bellasis 1845	
22	Kilmore	12	1702	Kilmore 1859		
23	Kinawley	3	Swanlinbar 1798 Trinity (Holy) 1842	Glangevlin 1867 Kinawley 1835		
24	Knockbride	21	1825	Knockbride 1835		S.P. Corronary 1764
25	Larah	20		Laragh 1876		
26	Lavey	15		Lavey 1867		
27	Loughan or Castlekeeran	36		Carnaross 1805		
28	Lurgan	33	1831	Lurgan 1755		
29	Moybolgue	25		Kilmainham & Moybologue 1867		
30	Mullagh	34		Mullagh 1842		
31	Munterconnaught	35		Castlerahan & Munterconnaught 1751		
32	Scrabby	9		Scrabby & Columcille East 1833		
33	Shercock	22		Killann 1835	Shercock or Glassleck	
34	Templeport	2		Templeport 1836 Glangevlin 1867 Corlough 1877		
35	Tomregan	5	1797	Kildallan & Tomregan 1867		
36	Urney	10		Urney & Annagelliffe 1812	Cavan 1851	M. Cavan

NGA No.	CIVIL PARISH	GV No.	CHURCH OF IRELAND	ROMAN CATHOLIC	PRESBYTERIAN	OTHERS
1	Abbey	3		Beagh 1849		
2	Bunratty	76		Newmarket 1828		
3	Carran	10		Carron (Kilcronin & Kilcorny) 1853		
4	Clareabbey	45		Clareabbey & Killone 1853		
5	Clondagad	46		Clondegad 1846		
6	Clonlea	49		O'Callaghan's Mills 1835		
7	Clonloghan	71		Newmarket 1828		
8	Clonrush	107 Galway		Clonrush 1846		
9	Clooney	18, 30		Ennistymon (Kilmanaheen & Clooney) 1870 Quin 1816		
10	Doora	31		Doora & Kilraghtis 1821		
11	Drumcliff	43	1744	Ennis 1837	Ennis	
12	Drumcreehy	2		Glanaragh 1854		
13	Drumline	72		Newmarket 1828		
14	Dysert	25		Dysart & Ruan 1845		
15	Feakle	33		Feakle Lower 1860 Killanena 1842		
16	Feenagh	73		Sixmilebridge 1828		
17	Gleninagh	1		Glanaragh 1854		
18	Inagh	24		Inagh & Kilnamona 1850		
19	Inchicronan	27		Crusheen 1860		
20	Inishcaltra	38, 106 Galway	1851	Clonrush 1846		
21	Kilballyowen	57		Kilballyowen (Cross) 1878		
22	Kilchreest	63		Clondegad 1846		
23	Kilconry	75		Newmarket 1828		
24	Kilcorney	9		Carron (Kilcronin & Kilcorny) 1853		

COUNTY CLARE

NGA No.	CIVIL PARISH	GV No.	CHURCH OF IRELAND	ROMAN CATHOLIC	PRESBYTERIAN	OTHERS
25	Kilfarboy	39		Kilfarboy 1831		
26	Kilfearagh	56	1842	Kilkee 1869		
27	Kilfenora	16		Kilfenora 1836		
28	Kilfiddane	62		Kilfidane 1868		
29	Kilfinaghta	74		Sixmilebridge 1828		
30	Kilfintinan	77		Sixmilebridge 1828		
31	Kilkeedy	20		Kilkeedy 1833		
32	Killadysert	64		Kildysart 1829		
33	Killaloe	53	1679	Killaloe 1828 Dooness & Trugh 1851		
34	Killard	41		Killard 1855 Kilkee 1869		
35	Killaspuglonane	14		Liscannor (Kilmacreehy & Killaspuglonane) 1843		
36	Killeany	8		Touclea (Killeany, Killymoon & Killileagh) 1854		
37	Killeely	78		Cratloe 1802		
38	Killilagh	12		Touclea (Killeany, Killymoon & Killileagh) 1854		
39	Killimer	65		Killimer 1859		
40	Killinaboy	21		Corofin 1818		
41	Killofin	66		Kilmurry-Mc Mahon 1837		
42	Killokennedy	51		Broadford 1844 Dooness & Trugh 1851		
43	Killonaghan	5		Glanaragh 1854		
44	Killone	44		Clareabbey & Killone 1853		
45	Killuran	48		O'Callaghan's Mills 1835		
46	Kilmacduane	55		Kilmacduane 1853		

13

COUNTY CLARE

NGA No.	CIVIL PARISH	GV No.	CHURCH OF IRELAND	ROMAN CATHOLIC	PRESBYTERIAN	OTHERS
47	Kilmacrehy	13		Liscannor (Kilmacreehy & Killaspuglonane) 1843		
48	Kilmaleery	70		Newmarket 1828		
49	Kilmaley	42		Inch & Kilmaley 1828		
50	Kilmanaheen	17		Ennistymon (Kilmanaheen & Clooney) 1870		
51	Kilmihil	60		Kilmihil 1849		
52	Kilmoon	6		Touclea (Killeany, Killymoon & Killileagh) 1854		
53	Kilmurry	40, 61, 69		Kilmurry-Ibrickane 1839 Kilmurry-Mc Mahon 1837 Sixmilebridge 1828		
54	Kilnamona	26		Inagh & Kilnamona 1850		
55	Kilnasoolagh	67	1731	Newmarket 1828		
56	Kilnoe	37		Kilnoe & Tuamgraney 1832		
57	Kilraghtis	29		Doora & Kilraghtis 1821		
58	Kilrush	59	1773	Kilrush 1827		
59	Kilseily	50		Broadford 1844		
60	Kilshanny	15		Kilshanny		
61	Kiltenanlea	54		Dooness & Trugh 1851		
62	Kiltoraght	19		Kilfenora 1836		
63	Moyarta	58		Carrigaholt 1852		
64	Moynoe	35		Scariff & Moynoe 1852		
65	Noughaval	11		Carron (Kilcronin & Kilcorny) 1853		
66	O'Briensbridge	52		Dooness & Trugh 1851 Killaloe 1828		

NGA No.	CIVIL PARISH	GV No.	CHURCH OF IRELAND	ROMAN CATHOLIC	PRESBYTERIAN	OTHERS
67	Ogonnelloe	47	1807	Ogonnelloe 1832		
68	Oughtmama	4		New Quay (Glan-amanagh) 1847 Beagh 1849		
69	Quin	32		Quin 1816		
70	Rath	22		Corofin 1818		
71	Rathborney	7		Glanaragh 1854		
72	Ruan	23		Dysart & Ruan 1845		
73	St. Munchin's	79		Cratloe 1802		
74	St. Patrick's	80		Parteen & Meelick 1814		
75	Templemaley	28		Doora & Kilraghtis 1821		
76	Tomfinlough	68		Newmarket 1828		
77	Tomgraney	34		Kilnoe & Tuam-graney 1832 Scariff & Moynoe 1852		
78	Tulla	36		Tulla 1819		

NGA No.	CIVIL PARISH	GV No.	CHURCH OF IRELAND	ROMAN CATHOLIC	PRESBYTERIAN	OTHERS
1	Aghacross	32A E		Kildorrery 1803		
2	Aghada	105 E	1815	Aghada 1815	Aghada 1863	
3	Aghern	69 E		Conna 1834		
4	Ardagh	87 E		Killeagh 1822		
5	Ardnageehy	42 E		Watergrasshill 1836		
6	Ballintemple	108 E		Cloyne 1786		
7	Ballycurrany	53 E		Lisgoold 1807		
8	Ballydeloher	59 E		Glounthaune 1864		
9	Ballydeloughy	12 E		Glountane 1829		
10	Ballyfeard	29 SW		Clonthead 1836		
11	Ballyfoyle	35 SW		Tracton Abbey 1802		
12	Ballyholly	27 E	1788	Castletownroche 1811		
13	Ballynoe	70 E		Conna 1834		
14	Ballyoughtera	94 E		Midleton 1819		
15	Ballyspillane	62 E		Midleton 1819		
17	Barnahely	41 SW		Passage West 1795		
18	Bohillane	99 E		Ballymacoda & Lady's Bridge 1835		
19	Bridgetown	25 E	1856	Castletownroche 1811		
20	Brigown	33 E	1775	Mitchelstown 1792		
21	Britway	50 E		Castlelyons 1791		
22	Caherlag	60 E		Glounthaune 1864		

NGA No.	CIVIL PARISH	GV No.	CHURCH OF IRELAND	ROMAN CATHOLIC	PRESBYTERIAN	OTHERS
23	Carrigaline	38 SW	1723 Douglas 1792	Carrigaline 1826 Douglas 1812 Passage West 1795		
24	Carrigdownane	13 E		Kildorrery 1803		
25	Carrigleamleary	15 E	1779	Annakissy 1805		
26	Carrigtohill	61 E	1776	Carrigtwohill 1817		
27	Castlelyons	44 E		Castlelyons 1791		
28	Castletownroche	17 E	1727	Castletownroche 1811		
29	Clenor	16 E	1813	Annakissy 1805		
30	Clondulane	38A E		Fermoy 1828		
31	Clonmel	66 E	or Queenstown 1761 Christ Church (Rushbrook) 1866	Cobh 1812	Cobh or Queenstown 1847	M. Queenstown
32	Clonmult	58 E		Imogeela 1833		
33	Clonpriest	91 E	1851 marriages	Killeagh 1822 Youghall 1801		
34	Cloyne	98 E	1708	Cloyne 1786		
35	Coole	45 E		Castlelyons 1791		
36	Corkbeg	107 E	1836	Aghada 1815		
37	Cork Holy Trinity	80 E	or Christ Church 1643 St. Luke 1837	St. Mary's 1748 St. Patrick's 1831	Cork – Trinity 1832 Queen Street 1862	M. Cork C. Cork B. Cork Q. Cork
38	Cork St. Nicholas	80 E	1721	St. Mary's 1748 St. Patrick's 1831		
39	Cork St. Paul's	80 E		St. Peter's & Paul's 1766		
40	Cork St. Peter's	80 E		St. Peter's & Paul's 1766		
41	Cullen	27 SW	1847	Clonthead 1836		

NGA No.	CIVIL PARISH	GV No.	CHURCH OF IRELAND	ROMAN CATHOLIC	PRESBYTERIAN	OTHERS
42	Dangandonovan	88 E		Killeagh 1822		
43	Derryvillane	11 E		Glanworth & Ballindangan 1836		
44	Doneraile	5 E	1730	Doneraile 1815		
45	Dunbulloge	41 E		Glanmire 1803 Watergrasshill 1836		
46	Dungourney	57 E	1817	Imogeela 1833		
47	Dunmahon	20 E		Glanworth & Ballindangan 1836		
48	Farahy	7 E	1765	Kildorrery 1803		
49	Fermoy	38 E	1801	Fermoy 1828	Fermoy (united with Lismore 1941)	
50	Garranekinnefeake	97 E	1856	Aghada 1815		
51	Garryvoe	100 E		Ballymacoda & Lady's Bridge 1835		
52	Glanworth	18 E	1805	Glanworth & Ballindangan 1836		
53	Gortroe	49 E		Rathcormac 1792		
54	Ightermurragh	95 E		Ballymacoda & Lady's Bridge 1835		
55	Inch	103 E	1815	Aghada 1815		
56	Inchinabacky	65 E		Midleton 1819		
57	Kilcredan	101 E		Ballymacoda & Lady's Bridge 1835		
58	Kilcrumper	21 E		Fermoy 1828 Kilworth 1829		
59	Kilcully	74 E		Glanmire 1803		
60	Kilcummer	26 E	1856	Castletownroche 1811		
61	Kildorrery	30 E		Kildorrery 1803		

NGA No.	CIVIL PARISH	GV No.	CHURCH OF IRELAND	ROMAN CATHOLIC	PRESBYTERIAN	OTHERS
62	Kilgullane	34 E		Glanworth & Ballindangan 1836		
63	Killanully	39 SW, 86 E	1831	Douglas 1812		
64	Killaspugmullane	51 E		Watergrasshill 1836		
65	Killathy	28 E		Castletownroche 1811		
66	Killeagh	90 E	1782	Killeagh 1822		
67	Killeenemer	19 E		Glanworth & Ballindangan 1836		
68	Kilmacdonagh	96 E		Ballymacoda & Lady's Bridge 1835		
69	Kilmahon	104 E	1773	Ballymacoda & Lady's Bridge 1835 Cloyne 1786		
70	Kilmoney	42 SW		Carrigaline 1826		
71	Kilmonoge	32 SW		Clonthead 1836		
72	Kilpatrick	31 SW		Tracton Abbey 1802		
73	Kilphelan	35 E		Mitchelstown 1792		
74	Kilquane	52 E		Glounthaune 1864 Watergrasshill 1836		
75	Kilshanahan	48 E		Watergrasshill 1836		
76	Kilworth	36 E	1776	Kilworth 1829		
77	Kinure	33 SW		Tracton Abbey 1802		
78	Knockmourne	68 E		Conna 1834		
79	Leitrim	39 E		Kilworth 1829		
80	Liscleary	40 SW		Douglas 1812 Passage West 1795		

NGA No.	CIVIL PARISH	GV No.	CHURCH OF IRELAND	ROMAN CATHOLIC	PRESBYTERIAN	OTHERS
81	Lisgoold	54 E	& Imphrick 1847	Lisgoold 1807		
82	Lismore & Mocollop	40 E		Lismore 1820		
83	Litter	29 E	1811	Fermoy 1828 Castletownroche 1811		
84	Little Island	63 E		Glounthaune 1864		
85	Macroney	37 E		Kilworth 1829		
86	Marmullane	36 SW	1801	Monkstown 1875		
87	Marshalstown	32 E		Mitchelstown 1792		
88	Middleton	93 E	or Roatellan 1810	Midleton 1819		
89	Mogeely	71 E		Conna 1834		
90	Mogeesha	64 E	1852	Carrigtwohill 1817 Midleton 1819		
91	Monanimy	24 E	1812	Annakissy 1805		
92	Monkstown	37 SW	1842	Monkstown 1875		
93	Nohaval	34 SW	1785	Tracton Abbey 1802		
94	Rahan	23 E	1773	Mallow 1757		
95	Rathcooney	73 E	1749	Glanmire 1803		
96	Rathcormack	43 E		Rathcormac 1792		
97	Rostellan	102 E	or Midleton 1810	Aghada 1815		
98	St. Anne's Shandon	77 E	1772	St. Mary's 1748 St. Patrick's 1831		
99	St. Finbar's	79 E	1752	Blackrock 1810 St. Finbar's 1756		
100	St. Michael's	46 E	Blackrock 1828	Glanmire 1803		
101	St. Nathlash	10 E	or St. Nicholas 1812	Kildorrery 1803		

NGA No.	CIVIL PARISH	GV No.	CHURCH OF IRELAND	ROMAN CATHOLIC	PRESBYTERIAN	OTHERS
102	Templebodan	55 E		Lisgoold 1807		
103	Templebreedy	43 SW		Carrigaline 1826		
104	Templemolaga	31 E		Kildorrery 1803		
105	Templenacarriga	56 E		Lisgoold 1807		
106	Templeroan	6 E		Doneraile 1815		
107	Templerobin	67 E		Cobh 1812		
108	Templeusque	47 E		Glanmire 1803		
109	Titeskin	106 E		Cloyne 1786		
110	Trabolgan	109 E		Aghada 1815		
111	Tracton	30 SW		Tracton Abbey 1802		
112	Wallstown	9 E	1829	Annakissy 1805		
113	Youghal	92 E	1665	Youghal 1801		C. Youghal Q. Youghal

NGA No.	CIVIL PARISH	GV No.	CHURCH OF IRELAND	ROMAN CATHOLIC	PRESBYTERIAN	OTHERS
1	Abbeymahon	66 SW	1827	Barryroe 1771		
2	Aghabulloge	48 NW	1808	Aghabullogue 1820		
3	Aghinagh	50 NW		Aghinagh 1848 Aghabullogue 1820 Macroom 1780		
4	Aglish	56 NW		Ovens 1816		
5	Aglishdrinagh	24 NW		Ballyhea 1809		
6	Ardskeagh	2 E		Ballyhea 1809 Charleville 1774		
7	Athnowen	57 NW		Ovens 1816		
8	Ballinaboy	70 NW, 85 E, 25 SW		Ballincollig 1820 Ballinhassig 1821		
9	Ballinadee	46 NW, 74 SW		Kilmurry 1786 Courcey's Country 1819		
10	Ballyclogh	34 NW	1795	Ballyclogh 1805		
11	Ballyhay	20 NW, 1 E	1728	Ballyhea 1809 Charleville 1774		
12	Ballymartle	26 SW	1785	Clonthead 1836		
13	Ballymodan	20 SW	1695	Bandon 1794	Bandon 1842	M. Bandon Q. Bandon
14	Bregoge	31 NW		Buttevant 1814		
15	Brinny	17 SW	1797	Innishannon 1825		
16	Buttevant	32 NW	1757	Buttevant 1814		
17	Caherduggan	8 E		Doneraile 1815		
18	Cannaway	55 NW		Kilmurry 1786		

NGA No.	CIVIL PARISH	GV No.	CHURCH OF IRELAND	ROMAN CATHOLIC	PRESBYTERIAN	OTHERS
19	Carrigrohane	64 NW 78 E		Ballincollig 1820		
20	Carrigrohanebeg	58 NW		Inniscarra 1814		
21	Castlemagner	10 NW	1810	Castlemagner 1832		
22	Churchetown	27 NW	1806	Liscarrol 1812		
23	Clondrohid	39 NW	1840 marriages	Clondrohid 1807 Kilnamartyra 1803		
24	Clonfert	1 NW	or Newmarket 1771	Newmarket 1821 Rock & Meelin 1866		
25	Clonmeen	13 NW	& Roskeen 1764	Castlemagner 1832 Clonmeen 1847		
26	Clontead	84 SW		Clonthead 1836		
27	Cooliney	23 NW		Ballyhea 1809		
28	Corbally	66 NW		Ballincollig 1820		
29	Corcomohide	18 NW		Ballyagran 1841		
30	Cullen	11 NW, 27 SW	1847	Dromtariffe 1832 Millstreet 1853 Clonthead 1836		
31	Currykippane	75 E		St. Peter's & Paul's 1766		
32	Desert	79 SW		Clonakilty & Darrara 1809		
33	Desertmore	61 NW		Ovens 1816		
34	Desertserges	71 SW	1837	Bandon 1794 Enniskeane & Desertserges 1813		
35	Donaghmore	49 NW, 68 SW		Donaghmore 1790 Barryroe 1771		
36	Drishane	36 NW	1792	Millstreet 1853		
37	Dromdowney	35 NW		Ballyclogh 1805		

23

NGA No.	CIVIL PARISH	GV No.	CHURCH OF IRELAND	ROMAN CATHOLIC	PRESBYTERIAN	OTHERS
38	Dromtarriff	12 NW	1825	Dromtariffe 1832		
39	Dunderrow	68 NW, 24 SW	1811 marriages	Ballincollig 1820 Ballinhassig 1821 Kinsale 1805		
40	Dunisky	44 NW		Kilmichael 1819		
41	Garrycloyne	54 NW		Blarney 1778		
42	Grenagh	72 NW		Grenagh 1840 Mourne Abbey 1829		
43	Hackmys	22 NW		Charleville 1774		
44	Imphrick	29 NW, 4 E	& Lisgoold 1847	Ballyhea 1809		
45	Inishannon	22 SW	1693	Innishannon 1825		
46	Inishcarra	52 NW	1820	Inniscarra 1814		
47	Inishkenny	69 NW, 83 E		Ballincollig 1820		
48	Kilbolane	17 NW	& Knocktemple 1779	Freemount 1827		
49	Kilbonane	60 NW		Kilmurry 1786		
50	Kilbrin	7 NW	& Liscarrol 1805	Ballyclogh 1805		
51	Kilbrittain	73 SW		Kilbritain 1810		
52	Kilbrogan	19 SW	1752	Bandon 1794 Murragh 1834		
53	Kilbroney	30 NW		Buttevant 1814		
54	Kilcorcoran	6 NW		Kanturk 1822		
55	Kilcorney	37 NW		Clonmeen 1847		
56	Kilgrogan	28 NW		Liscarrol 1812		
57	Killowen	18 SW	1833	Murragh 1834		

NGA No.	CIVIL PARISH	GV No.	CHURCH OF IRELAND	ROMAN CATHOLIC	PRESBYTERIAN	OTHERS
58	Kilmaclenine	33 NW		Ballyclogh 1805		
59	Kilmaloda	72 SW		Timoleague & Cloghagh 1842		
60	Kilmeen	5 NW	1806	Boherbue 1833 Dromtariffe 1832		
61	Kilmurry	47 NW	1832	Kilmurry 1786		
62	Kilnaglory	63 NW, 82 E		Ballincollig 1820		
63	Kilnagross	77 SW		Clonakilty & Darrara 1809		
64	Kilquane	3 E		Kilmallock 1837		
65	Kilroan	82 SW		Courcey's Country 1819		
66	Kilroe	8 NW	Kanturk 1818	Kanturk 1822		
67	Kilshannig	16 NW	1731	Glountane 1829		
68	Kilsillagh	69 SW		Barryroe 1771		
69	Kinsale	85 SW	1684	Kinsale 1805		M. Kinsale Q. Kinsale
70	Knockavilly	67 NW, 21 SW	1837	Innishannon 1825		
71	Knocktemple	3 NW	& Kilbolane 1779	Freemount 1827		
72	Lackeen	26 NW		Liscarrol 1812		
73	Leighmoney	28 SW		Innishannon 1825		
74	Liscarroll	25 NW	& Kilbrin 1805	Liscarrol 1812		
75	Lislee	67 SW	1809	Barryroe 1771		
76	Macloneigh	43 NW		Kilmichael 1819		
77	Macroom	41 NW	1727	Macroom 1780 Aghinagh 1848 Aghabullogue 1820		

NGA No.	CIVIL PARISH	GV No.	CHURCH OF IRELAND	ROMAN CATHOLIC	PRESBYTERIAN	OTHERS
78	Magourney	51 NW	1757	Aghabullogue 1820		
79	Mallow	15 NW, 14 E	1776	Mourne Abbey 1829 Mallow 1757	Mallow	M. Mallow
80	Matehy	53 NW		Inniscarra 1814		
81	Mourneabbey	71 NW, 22 E	or Ballesanona 1807	Mourne Abbey 1829 Mallow 1757		
82	Moviddy	59 NW		Kilmurry 1786		
83	Murragh	15 SW	1754	Murragh 1834		
84	Nohavaldaly	4 NW		Boherbue 1833 Knocknacoppel or Kilcummin East 1821 Rathmore 1837		
85	Rathclarin	78 SW		Kilbritain 1810		
86	Rathgoggan	21 NW		Charleville 1774		Q. Charleville
87	Ringcurran	86 SW	1793	Kinsale 1805		
88	Ringrone	81 SW		Courcey's Country 1819		
89	Rosskeen	14 NW	& Clonmeen 1764	Castlemagner 1832		
90	St. Finbar's	62 NW		Ovens 1816		
91	St. Mary's Shandon	76 E	1671	St. Peter's & Paul's 1766		
92	St. Nicholas	65 NW, 81 E		Ballincollig 1820		
93	Shandrum	19 NW		Shandrum 1829 Ballyhea 1809 Charleville 1774 Freemount 1827		
94	Subulter	9 NW		Castlemagner 1832		
95	Templebryan	76 SW		Clonakilty & Darrara 1809		

NGA No.	CIVIL PARISH	GV No.	CHURCH OF IRELAND	ROMAN CATHOLIC	PRESBYTERIAN	OTHERS
96	Templemartin	16 SW	1806	Murragh 1834		
97	Templemichael	23 SW		Innishannon 1825		
98	Templeomalus	63 SW		Clonakilty & Darrara 1809		
99	Templequinlan	64 SW		Clonakilty & Darrara 1809		
100	Templetrine	80 SW		Courcey's Country 1819		
101	Timoleague	65 SW	1823	Timoleague & Cloghagh 1842		
102	Tisaxon	83 SW		Kinsale 1805		
103	Tullylease	2 NW	1850	Freemount 1827		
104	Whitechurch	73 NW, 72 E		Blarney 1778		

NGA No.	CIVIL PARISH	GV No.	CHURCH OF IRELAND	ROMAN CATHOLIC	PRESBYTERIAN	OTHERS
1	Abbeystrowry	52 SW	1778	Caheragh 1818 Aughadown 1822 Skibbereen 1814		
2	Aghadown	55 SW		Aughadown 1822		
3	Ardfield	61 SW	1835	Ardfield & Rathbarry 1800		
4	Ballymoney	70 SW	1805	Dunmanway 1818 Enniskeane & Desertserges 1813		
5	Ballyvourney	38 NW		Ballyvourney 1825 Kilnamartyra 1803		
6	Caheragh	46 SW	1836	Caheragh 1818		
7	Castlehaven	53 SW		Castlehaven 1842		
8	Castleventry	13 SW		Kilmeen & Castleventry 1821		
9	Clear Island	58 SW		Rath & Islands 1818		
10	Creagh	56 SW		Skibbereen 1814		M. Skibbereen Q. Skibbereen
11	Drinagh	51 SW		Drimoleague 1817		
12	Dromdaleague	50 SW	1812	Drimoleague 1817		
13	Durrus	45 SW		Muintervara 1819		
14	Fanlobbus	9 SW	(Dunmanway) 1855	Dunmanway 1818		
15	Inchigeelagh	42 NW, 6 SW		Iveleary 1816		
16	Island	62 SW		Ardfield & Rathbarry 1800 Clonakilty & Darrara 1809		
17	Kilcaskan	2 SW	Glengariffe (Holy Trinity) 1863	Adrigole 1830 Bonane 1846		
18	Kilcatherine	1 SW		Eyeries 1824		
19	Kilcoe	48 SW		Aughadown 1822		

NGA No.	CIVIL PARISH	GV No.	CHURCH OF IRELAND	ROMAN CATHOLIC	PRESBYTERIAN	OTHERS
20	Kilcrohane	44 SW		Muintervara 1819		
21	Kilfaughnabeg	14 SW		Kilmacabea 1832 Roscarberry & Lissevard 1814		
22	Kilgarriff	75 SW		Clonakilty & Darrara 1809	Clonakilty 1859 (united with Bandon 1919)	
23	Kilkerranmore	59 SW		Roscarberry & Lissevard 1814		
24	Killaconenagh	4 SW	Berehaven 1787	Castletownbere 1819		
25	Kilmacabea	11 SW		Kilmacabea 1832		
26	Kilmeen	10 SW		Kilmeen & Castleventry 1821		
27	Kilmichael	45 NW, 7 SW		Kilmichael 1819		
28	Kilmocomoge	5 SW		Bantry 1788		
29	Kilmoe	49 SW		Goleen (West Schull) 1827		
30	Kilnamanagh	3 SW		Castletownbere 1819 Allihies 1822		
31	Kilnamartery	40 NW		Kilnamartyra 1803		
32	Kinneigh	8 SW	1795	Murragh 1834 Enniskeane & Desertserges 1813		
33	Myross	54 SW		Castlehaven 1842		
34	Rathbarry	60 SW		Ardfield & Rathbarry 1800		
35	Ross	12 SW	Ross Cathedral 1690	Roscarberry & Lissevard 1814		
36	Skull	47 SW	Ballydehob 1826	East Schull 1807 Goleen (West Schull) 1827		
37	Tullagh	57 SW		Rath & Islands 1818 Skibbereen 1814		

COUNTY DONEGAL

NGA No.	CIVIL PARISH	GV No.	CHURCH OF IRELAND	ROMAN CATHOLIC	PRESBYTERIAN	OTHERS
1	Aghanunshin	18		Aughnish & Aghaninshin 1873		
2	All Saints	29	1820 burials	All Saints, Raymorky & Taughboyne 1843	Newtown-cunningham 1830	
3	Aughnish	16	Tullyaughnish 1798	Aughnish & Aghaninshin 1873 Killygarvan & Tullyfern 1868	Ray – 1st 2nd (united 1927)	
4	Burt	25	1802	Burt, Inch & Fahan 1856	Burt 1833	
5	Clonca	1		Clonca 1856	Malin	
6	Clondahorky	10		Clondahorky 1877	Dunfanaghy 1873	
7	Clondavaddog	7	1794	Clonvaddog 1847		
8	Clonleigh	35	1863	Clonleigh 1773	Ballindrait 1819	
9	Clonmany	2		Clonmany 1852		
10	Convoy	36		Raphoe 1876	Convoy 1822	R.P. Convoy
11	Conwal	17		Conwal & Leck 1853	Letterkenny – 1st & 3rd 1841 (united 1925) 2nd (dissolved 1858) Trenta 1836	R.P. Gortlea B. Letterkenny Q. Letterkenny
12	Culdaff	4		Clonca 1856 Culdaff 1838		
13	Desertegny	20		Desertegny & Lower Fahan 1864		
14	Donagh	3		Donagh 1847	Carndonagh	
15	Donaghmore	39	Meenglass 1864 Monellan 1863	Donaghmore 1840	Donoughmore 1844 Carnone 1834	
16	Donegal	48	1803	Tawnawilly 1872	Donegal – 1st & 2nd 1825 (united 1884)	M. Donegal C. Donegal
17	Drumhome	49	1691	Drumhome 1866		
18	Fahan Lower	21	1817	Desertegny & Lower Fahan 1864	Buncrana 1836	
19	Fahan Upper	22	1761	Burt, Inch & Fahan 1856	Fahan	

30

NGA No.	CIVIL PARISH	GV No.	CHURCH OF IRELAND	ROMAN CATHOLIC	PRESBYTERIAN	OTHERS
20	Gartan	14		Termon & Gartan 1862		
21	Glencolumbkille	42	1827	Glencolumbkille 1880		
22	Inch	24	1858	Burt, Inch & Fahan 1856	Inch	
23	Inishkeel	28	1826 Glenties 1829 marriages	Ardara 1867 Inishkeel (Glenties) 1866 Kincassligh (Burtonport)		
24	Inishmacsaint	52	Finner 1815	Magh Ene (Bundoran) 1847		
25	Inver	46	1805	Inver 1861		
26	Kilbarron	51	1785	Kilbarron 1854	Ballyshannon 1836	M. Ballyshannon
27	Kilcar	43	1819	Kilcar 1848		
28	Killaghtee	45	1810	Killaghtee 1845		
29	Killea	33		All Saints, Raymorky & Taughboyne 1843		
30	Killybegs Lower	41	Ardara 1829	Ardara 1867		
31	Killybegs Upper	44	Killybegs 1787	Killybegs 1850		
32	Killygarvan	13		Killygarvan & Tullyfern 1868	Rathmullan 1854	
33	Killymard	47		Killymard 1874		
34	Kilmacrenan	15		Kilmacrenan 1862	Kilmacrenan	
35	Kilteevoge	37	1818	Kilteevogue 1855		
36	Leck	30		Conwal & Leck 1853		
37	Lettermacaward	27		Lettermacaward & Templecrone 1876		
38	Mevagh	11		Mevagh 1871	Carrigart & Creeslough 1844	
39	Mintiaghs or Barr of Inch	19		Desertegny & Lower Fahan 1864		
40	Moville Lower	5		Moville Lower 1847	Moville 1834 Greenbank 1862 (united with Moville 1959)	
41	Moville Upper	6	1812	Iskaheen & Moville Upper 1858		

NGA No.	CIVIL PARISH	GV No.	CHURCH OF IRELAND	ROMAN CATHOLIC	PRESBYTERIAN	OTHERS
42	Muff	23	1803	Iskaheen & Moville Upper 1858	Knowhead or Muff 1826	
43	Raphoe	34	1831	Raphoe 1876	Raphoe – 1st 1829 2nd 1829	
44	Raymoghy	31		All Saints, Raymorky & Taughboyne 1843		
45	Raymunterdoney	9		Clondahorky 1877 Tullaghobegley East, Raymunterdoney & Trory 1849		
46	Stranorlar	38	1821	Stranorlar 1860	Stranorlar 1821	
47	Taughboyne	32	1819	All Saints, Raymorky & Taughboyne 1843	Monreagh 1845 Saint Johnstown 1838 Crossroads 1855 Ballylennon 1829	
48	Templecarn	50	1825	Carn 1836	Pettigoe	
49	Templecrone	26		Annagry 1868 Lettermacaward & Templecrone 1876 Gweedore 1868		
50	Tullaghobegley	8	1821	Gweedore 1868 Tullaghobegley East, Raymunterdoney & Trory 1849		
51	Tullyfern	12		Killygarvan & Tullyfern 1868	Ramelton – 1st 1806 2nd 1808 3rd 1839 Milford 1839 Fannet 1859	R.P. Milford M. Ramelton
52	Urney	40		Urney	Alt	

NGA No.	CIVIL PARISH	GV No.	CHURCH OF IRELAND	ROMAN CATHOLIC	PRESBYTERIAN	OTHERS
1	Aghaderg	50	1814	Aghaderg 1816	Scarva 1807 Fourtowns 1822 Loughbrickland 1842 Poyntzpass 1850	
2	Annaclone	51		Annaclone 1834	Anaghlone – 1st & 2nd 1839 (united 1890)	
3	Annahilt	36	1784	Ballynahinch 1827	Annahilt 1779 Cargycreevy	
4	Ardglass	48		Dunsford 1848		
5	Ardkeen	13	1745	Ardkeen 1828		
6	Ardquin	15		Ballyphilip 1843		
7	Ballee	45	1792	Ballyculter & Ballee 1843		S.P. Ballee
8	Ballyculter	44	1777	Ballyculter & Ballee 1843 Kilclief & Strangford 1865	Strangford 1846	
9	Ballyhalbert alias St. Andrew	12	1846	Ballyphilip 1843	Glastry 1728	S.P. Bally-hemlin M. Glastry 1879
10	Ballykinler	66		Tyrella & Dundrum 1854		
11	Ballyphilip	18	1745	Ballyphilip 1843	Portaferry 1699	
12	Ballytrustan	16		Ballyphilip 1843		
13	Ballywalter alias Whitechurch	10	1844	Ballygalget 1828	Ballywalter – 1st 1824 2nd 1820 (united 1925)	
14	Bangor	7	1803	Bangor 1855	Bangor – 1st 1852 2nd or Trinity 1833 Groomsport 1841 Ballygilbert 1841 Ballygrainey 1838 Conlig 1845	B. Conlig
15	Blaris	31		Blaris (Lisburn) 1840	Lisburn – 1st 1692 Railway Street 1860 Maze 1856	S.P. Lisburn, Sloan Street 1861 M. Lisburn Q. Lisburn

COUNTY DOWN

NGA No.	CIVIL PARISH	GV No.	CHURCH OF IRELAND	ROMAN CATHOLIC	PRESBYTERIAN	OTHERS
16	Bright	69		Bright 1856		
17	Castleboy	14		Ardkeen 1828		
18	Clonallan	54	1825	Clonallon 1826		S.P. Narrow-water
19	Clonduff	62	1782	Clonduff 1850	Clonduff 1842 Hilltown 1845 (united with Clonduff 1964)	
20	Comber	4	1683	Newtownards, Comber & Donaghadee 1864	Comber – 1st 1847 2nd 1849 Ballygowan 1860	S.P. Money-reagh 1838 S.P. Comber M. Comber 1870
21	Donaghadee	8	1771	Newtownards, Comber & Donaghadee 1864	Donaghadee – 1st 1805 2nd 1849 Millisle 1773 Ballyfrenis 1863 Carrowdore 1843	M. Donaghadee 1827
22	Donaghcloney	33	1697	Tullylish 1833	Donacloney 1798 Waringstown 1862.	
23	Donaghmore	52	1783	Donaghmore 1825	Donaghmore 1804 Jerretspass or 2nd Drum-banagher 1832 (united with 1st Drum-banagher 1902)	
24	Down	65	Downpatrick 1733	Downpatrick 1851	Downpatrick 1827	S.P. Down-patrick M. Down-patrick 1829.
25	Dromara	58		Dromara 1844 Ballynahinch 1827	Dromara – 1st 1763 2nd 1853	
26	Dromore	35	1784	Dromore & Garvaghy 1821	Dromore – 1st 1857 2nd 1851 Drumlough 1827	R.P. Dromore 1845 M. Dromore 1832
27	Drumballyroney	59	1831	Annaclone 1834	Ballyroney 1819 Katesbridge 1866 Brookvale 1891 Glascar 1780	
28	Drumbeg	22	1807	Blaris (Lisburn) 1840	Hillhall 1866 Legacurry 1845	

34

COUNTY DOWN

NGA No.	CIVIL PARISH	GV No.	CHURCH OF IRELAND	ROMAN CATHOLIC	PRESBYTERIAN	OTHERS
29	Drumbo	23	1791	Blaris (Lisburn) 1840	Drumbo 1764 Ballycairn 1860 Carryduff 1854	
30	Drumgath	53		Drumgath 1829	Rathfriland – 1st 1763 2nd 1804 3rd 1834 (2nd & 3rd united 1927)	Q. Rathfriland
31	Drumgooland	60	1779	Drumgooland Lower 1832 Drumgooland Upper 1827	Drumgooland 1833 Drumlee 1826	B. Derryneil 1869
32	Dundonald	2	1811	Newtownards, Comber & Donaghadee 1864	Dundonald 1678	
33	Dunsfort	47		Dunsford 1848		
34	Garvaghy	57		Dromore & Garvaghy 1821	Garvaghy 1809 Kilkinamurry	
35	Grey Abbey	9	1807	Ballygalget 1828	Grey Abbey 1875	R.P. Grey Abbey
36	Hillsborough	30	1763	Blaris (Lisburn) 1840	Hillsborough 1833 Loughaghery 1803	Q. Hillsborough
37	Holywood	1	1806 Dundela 1864	Holywood 1866	Holywood – 1st 1840 2nd 1857	M. Holywood 1867
38	Inch	42	1767	Kilmore		
39	Inishargy	11	1783 Kircubbin 1847	Ballyphilip 1843	Kircubbin 1778	
40	Kilbroney	56	1814	Kilbroney 1808	Rostrevor 1851	Q. Newtown
41	Kilclief	46	1860	Kilclief & Strangford 1865		
42	Kilcoo	63	1786 Newcastle 1843	Kilcoo 1832 Maghera & Bryansford 1845	Newcastle	M. Newcastle 1881
43	Kilkeel	71	1816 Annalong 1842	Kilkeel 1839 Mourne Lower 1839	Kilkeel 1840 Annalong 1840 Mourne 1840	
44	Killaney	25	1857	Carrickmannon & Saintfield 1837	Killaney 1846 Boardmills – 1st 1782 2nd 1846 (united with Killaney 1925 and with 1st Boardmills 1974)	
45	Killinchy	26	1819	Carrickmannon & Saintfield 1837	Killinchy 1812 Raffrey 1843	R.P. Killinchy R.P. Ravara

NGA No.	CIVIL PARISH	GV No.	CHURCH OF IRELAND	ROMAN CATHOLIC	PRESBYTERIAN	OTHERS
46	Killyleagh	27	1813	Kilmore	Killyleagh – 1st 1693 2nd 1840	
47	Kilmegan	61	1823	Drumaroad 1853 Kilmegan 1859	Castlewellan 1845 Drumaroad & Clanvaraghan 1853 Leitrim 1837	M. Dundrum 1881
48	Kilmood	5	1822	Newtownards, Comber & Donaghadee 1864		
49	Kilmore	40	1820	Kilmore	Kilmore 1833 Lissara 1809	S.P. Rademon 1830
50	Knockbreda	20	1784 Ballymacarrett 1827 St. John, Orangefield 1853	Ballymacarrett 1841	Ballymacarrett 1837 Mountpottinger or 2nd Bally- macarrett 1867 Gilnahirk 1797 Newtownbreda 1845 Castlereagh 1809 Granshaw	
51	Lambeg	21	1810	Blaris (Lisburn) 1840		
52	Loughinisland	41	1760	Loughinisland 1805	Seaforde 1836 Clough 1836	
53	Maghera	64		Maghera & Bryansford 1845		
54	Magheradrool	38		Ballynahinch 1827	Ballynahinch – 1st 1841 2nd 1829 3rd 1820 (2nd & 3rd united 1927)	M. Ballynahinch 1879
55	Magherahamlet	39		Ballynahinch 1827	Magherahamlet 1831	
56	Magheralin	32	1692	Magheralin 1815		
57	Magherally	37		Tullylish 1833	Magherally 1837	
58	Moira	29	1725	Magheralin 1815	Moira 1866	S.P. Moira M. Moira 1827
59	Newry	70	1807	Newry 1818	Newry – 1st or Sandys Street 1829 2nd or Down- shire Road 1849 3rd or River- side 1863 (dissolved 1883) Ryans 1851	R.P. Newry M. Newry 1830 C. Newry

NGA No.	CIVIL PARISH	GV No.	CHURCH OF IRELAND	ROMAN CATHOLIC	PRESBYTERIAN	OTHERS
60	Newtownards	3		Newtownards, Comber & Donaghadee 1864	Newtownards - 1st 1833 2nd 1834 Regent Street 1835 Strean 1867 Greenwell Street 1869 Ballyblack 1854	S.P. Newtown- ards 1827 M. Newtownards 1870
61	Rathmullan	68		Bright 1856		
62	Saintfield	24	1724	Carrickmannon & Saintfield 1837	Saintfield - 1st 1851 2nd 1831	
63	Saul	43		Ballyculter & Ballee 1843 Saul 1868		
64	Seapatrick	49	1802	Tullylish 1833 Banbridge 1843	Bannbridge - Scarva Street 1756 Bannside 1867 Ballydown 1804	S.P. Banbridge B. Banbridge
65	Shankhill	28	1681	Magheralin 1815		
66	Slanes	17		Ballyphilip 1843	Cloughey 1841	
67	Tullylish	34	1820 Gilford 1869 Knocknamuckley 1838	Tullylish 1833	Tullylish 1813 Gilford 1843 Newmills 1838	M. Gilford 1836 Q. Moyallon
68	Tullynakill	6	1847	Newtownards, Comber & Donaghadee 1864		
69	Tyrella	67	1839	Tyrella & Dundrum 1854		
70	Warrenpoint	55	1825	Clonallon 1826	Warrenpoint 1832	M. Warrenpoint 1878

NGA No.	CIVIL PARISH	GV No.	CHURCH OF IRELAND	ROMAN CATHOLIC	PRESBYTERIAN	OTHERS
1	Aderrig	49		Clondalkin, Lucan & Palmerston 1778		
2	Artaine	39		Clontarf, Coolock, Santry & Artane 1774		
3	Baldongan	5		Skerries 1751		
4	Baldoyle	36		Baldoyle, Howth, Kilbarrack & Kinsaley 1784		
5	Balgriffin	34		Baldoyle, Howth, Kilbarrack & Kinsaley 1784		
6	Ballyboghil	14		Naul		
7	Ballyfermot	59		Clondalkin, Lucan & Palmerston 1778		
8	Ballymadun	10		Garristown & Ballymadun 1857		
9	Balrothery	2	Balbriggan 1838	Balbriggan (Balrothery) 1816		
10	Balscaddan	1		Balbriggan (Balrothery) 1816		
11	Booterstown	71	1824	Booterstown, Blackrock & Dundrum 1755		
12	Castleknock	26	1709	Blanchardstown 1774		
13	Chapelizod	27	1812	Blanchardstown 1774		
14	Cloghran	23, 31	1732	Blanchardstown 1774 Swords 1763		
15	Clondalkin	58	1728	Clondalkin, Lucan & Palmerston 1778		
16	Clonmethan	12		Rolleston 1857		
17	Clonsilla	25	1830	Blanchardstown 1774		
18	Clontarf	46	1807	Clontarf, Coolock, Santry & Artane 1774	Clontarf 1836	

NGA No.	CIVIL PARISH	GV No.	CHURCH OF IRELAND	ROMAN CATHOLIC	PRESBYTERIAN	OTHERS
19	Clonturk	38		Clontarf, Coolock, Santry & Artane 1774		
20	Coolock	35	1760	Clontarf, Coolock, Santry & Artane 1774		
21	Cruagh	66		Rathfarnham 1771		
22	Crumlin	62	St. Mary's, Crumlin 1740	Rathfarnham 1771	Donore 1860	
23	Dalkey	78		Kingstown (Dun Laoghaire) 1769		
24	Donabate	17	1811	Donabate & Portane 1760		
25	Donnybrook	68	St. Mary's, Donnybrook 1712 Irishtown or St. Matthew's, Ringsend 1812 St. John, Sandymount 1850 Baggotrath 1865	Booterstown, Blackrock & Dundrum 1755 Donnybrook & Irishtown 1798	Sandymount 1857	
26	Drimnagh	61		Clodalkin, Lucan & Palmerston 1778		
27	Dublin City		See DUBLIN CITY	See DUBLIN CITY	Abbey 1779 Ormond Quay 1787 Adelaide Street 1840 Brunswick Street Mission Church 1854 Scots Church 1863	M. Dublin C. Dublin B. Dublin Q. Dublin
28	Esker	50		Clondalkin, Lucan & Palmerston 1778		
29	Finglas	24	1664 burials	Finglas & St. Margaret's 1757		
30	Garristown	7		Garristown & Ballymadun 1857		
31	Glasnevin	37	1778	Clontarf, Coolock, Santry & Artane 1774 St. Paul's 1731 St. Michan's 1726		

NGA No.	CIVIL PARISH	GV No.	CHURCH OF IRELAND	ROMAN CATHOLIC	PRESBYTERIAN	OTHERS
32	Grallagh	8		Naul		
33	Grangegorman	43		St. Paul's 1731		
34	Hollywood	9		Naul		
35	Holmpatrick	3	1779	Skerries 1751		
36	Howth	42	1804	Baldoyle, Howth, Kilbarrack & Kinsaley 1784	Howth & Malahide	
37	Kilbarrack	41		Baldoyle, Howth, Kilbarrack & Kinsaley 1784		
38	Kilbride	53		Clondalkin, Lucan & Palmerston 1778		
39	Kilgobbin	79		Sandyford 1857		
40	Kill	77		Booterstown, Blackrock & Dundrum 1755 Kingstown (Dun Laoghaire) 1769		
41	Killeek	20		Finglas & St. Margaret's 1757		
42	Killester	45		Clontarf, Coolock, Santry & Artane 1774		
43	Killiney	80		Kingstown (Dun Laoghaire) 1769		
44	Killossery	15		Rolleston 1857		
45	Kilmactalway	51		Clondalkin, Lucan & Palmerston 1778		
46	Kilmacud	73		Booterstown, Blackrock & Dundrum 1755		
47	Kilmahuddrick	52		Clondalkin, Lucan & Palmerston 1778		
48	Kilsallaghan	19	1818	Finglas & St. Margaret's 1757 Rolleston 1857		

NGA No.	CIVIL PARISH	GV No.	CHURCH OF IRELAND	ROMAN CATHOLIC	PRESBYTERIAN	OTHERS
49	Kiltiernan	81	1817	Sandyford 1857		
50	Kinsaley	32		Baldoyle, Howth, Kilbarrack & Kinsaley 1784		
51	Leixlip	47		Maynooth & Leixlip 1806		
52	Lucan	48		Clondalkin, Lucan & Palmerston 1778	Lucan 1876	
53	Lusk	4	1809 Kenure 1867	Lusk 1757 Rush 1785 Skerries 1751		
54	Malahide	28	1822	Swords 1763	Howth & Malahide	
55	Monkstown	75	1669 Mariner's Church Kingstown 1843 Kingstown (Christ Church) 1852 Carysfort (Blackrock) 1855 St. John, Monkstown 1860	Kingstown (Dun Laoghaire) 1769 Booterstown, Blackrock & Dundrum 1755	Kingstown or Dun Laoghaire	M. Kingstown
56	Mulhuddart	22		Blanchardstown 1774		
57	Naul	6		Naul		
58	Newcastle	54	Newcastle–Lyons 1773	Saggart 1832		
59	Oldconnaught	83		Kingstown (Dun Laoghaire) 1769		
60	Palmerston	57		Clondalkin, Lucan & Palmerston 1778		
61	Palmerstown	11		Rolleston 1857		
62	Portmarnock	33		Baldoyle, Howth, Kilbarrack & Kinsaley 1784		
63	Portraine	18		Donabate & Portrane 1760		
64	Raheny	40	1815	Clontarf, Coolock, Santry & Artane 1774		
65	Rathcoole	55		Saggart 1832		

COUNTY DUBLIN

NGA No.	CIVIL PARISH	GV No.	CHURCH OF IRELAND	ROMAN CATHOLIC	PRESBYTERIAN	OTHERS
66	Rathfarnham	69		Rathfarnham 1771 Booterstown, Blackrock & Dundrum 1755	Rathgar 1860	
67	Rathmichael	82	1865	Kingstown (Dun Laoghaire) 1769 Sandyford 1857		
68	Saggart	56		Saggart 1832		
69	St. Margaret's	29		Finglas & St. Margaret's 1757		
70	St. Peter's	64	& St. Kevin 1699 St. Peter's, Rathmines 1671 St. Philip, Milltown 1844 Holy Trinity, Rathmines 1850	St. Andrew's 1742 St. Michael's & John's 1743 St. Nicholas' Without 1742 Donnybrook & Irishtown 1798		
71	Santry	30	1753	Clontarf, Coolock, Santry & Artane 1774		
72	Stillorgan	74	All Saints, Newtown Park 1870	Booterstown, Blackrock & Dundrum 1755 Sandyford 1857		
73	Swords	16	1705	Swords 1763		
74	Tallaght	65		Rathfarnham 1771		
75	Taney	70	1835 Sandford 1826	Booterstown, Blackrock & Dundrum 1755 Donnybrook & Irishtown 1798		
79	Tully	76		Kingstown (Dun Laoghaire) 1769		
77	Ward	21		Finglas & St. Margaret's 1757		
78	Westpalstown	13		Naul		
79	Whitechurch	72	1824	Rathfarnham 1771		

NGA No.	CIVIL PARISH	GV No.	CHURCH OF IRELAND	ROMAN CATHOLIC	PRESBYTERIAN	OTHERS
1	Donnybrook	68	St. Mary's, Donnybrook 1712 Irishtown or St. Matthew's, Ringsend 1812 St. John, Sandymount 1850 Baggotrath 1865	Booterstown, Blackrock & Dundrum 1755 Donnybrook & Irishtown 1798	Sandymount 1857	
	DUBLIN CITY					
2	Christ Church		1740	St. Nicholas' Without 1742		
3	St. Andrew's		1672 marriages	St. Andrew's 1742 St. Michael's & John's 1743		
4	St. Anne's		1719 marriages St. Stephen's 1826	St. Andrew's 1742		
5	St. Audoen's		1673	St. Audoen's 1747		
6	St. Bartholomew's		1868 Christ Church, Leeson Park 1867	Donnybrook & Irishtown 1798		
7	St. Bridget's		1632	St. Michael's & John's 1743 St. Nicholas' Without 1742		
8	St. Catherine's	63	1636	St. Catherine's 1740		
9	St. George's	44	1794 Rotunda Chapel 1860	St. Mary's 1734 St. Michan's 1726		
10	St. James'	60	1742 Royal Hospital, Kilmainham 1826 St. Jude, Kilmainham 1857	St. James' 1752		
11	St. John's		1619	St. Michael's & John's 1743		
12	St. Luke's		1716 marriages	St. Nicholas' Without 1742		
13	St. Mark's	67	1730	St. Andrew's 1742 Donnybrook & Irishtown 1798		
14	St. Mary's		1697 marriages	St. Mary's 1734 St. Michan's 1726		
15	St. Michael's		1656 marriages	St. Michael's & John's 1743		

NGA No.	CIVIL PARISH	GV No.	CHURCH OF IRELAND	ROMAN CATHOLIC	PRESBYTERIAN	OTHERS
16	St. Michan's		1636	St. Michan's 1726 St. Paul's 1731		
17	St. Nicholas' Within		1671	St. Michael's & John's 1743 St. Nicholas' Without 1742		
18	St. Nicholas' Without		1694	St. Nicholas' Without 1742		
19	St. Patrick's		1677 St. Matthias 1851	St. Nicholas' Without 1742		
20	St. Paul's		1698	St. Paul's 1731 St. Michan's 1726		
21	St. Peter's	64	& St. Kevin 1699 St. Peter's, Rathmines 1671 St. Philip, Milltown 1844 Holy Trinity, Rathmines 1850	St. Andrew's 1742 St. Michael's & John's 1743 St. Nicholas' Without 1742 Donnybrook & Irishtown 1798		
22	St. Thomas'		1750	St. Mary's 1734		
23	St. Werburgh's		1704	St. Michael's & John's 1743		

NGA No.	CIVIL PARISH	GV No.	CHURCH OF IRELAND	ROMAN CATHOLIC	PRESBYTERIAN	OTHERS
1	Aghalurcher	17	1788 Lisnaskea 1804 Maguire's Bridge 1840 Mullaghfad 1836	Aghalurcher (Lisnaskea) 1835	Cavanaleck (Fivemiletown) 1836 Maguire's Bridge 1845	M. Maguire's Bridge 1872 M. Lisnaskea 1873
2	Aghavea	16	1815	Aghavea 1862		M. Brook-borough 1841
3	Belleek	2	1822	Pettigo (Carn) 1836		M. Belleek 1877
4	Boho.	13	1840	Derrygonnelly 1853 Inishmacsaint 1847		
5	Clones	18	Aghadrumsee 1821	Clones 1821 Roslea 1862		
6	Cleenish	14		Cleenish 1835 Enniskillen 1818	Lisbellaw 1849	M. Lisbellaw 1872
7	Derrybrusk	11		Enniskillen 1818		
8	Derryvullan	5	Derryvollan North 1803	Irvinestown 1846 Enniskillen 1818	Irvinestown (or Lowtherstown) 1842 (united with Pettigo 1908)	M. Irvinestown 1829
9	Devenish	7	1800	Derrygonnelly 1853 Garrison 1860 Inishmacsaint 1847		
10	Drumkeeran	1	1801 Coolaghty or Lack 1835	Magheraculmany (Ederny) 1836	Pettigo 1844	M. Pettigo 1870
11	Drumully	23	1802	Galloon (Newtownbutler) 1847		
12	Enniskillen	12	1666 Tempo 1836 Clabby 1862	Enniskillen 1818 Tempo 1845	Enniskillen 1837 Tempo 1874	M. Enniskillen 1823 M. Pubble 1872 M. Clabby 1879
13	Galloon	22	1798	Galloon (Newtownbutler) 1847		M. Newtown-butler 1873
14	Inishmacsaint	6	1813	Inishmacsaint 1847 Garrison 1860 Derrygonnelly 1853		M. Derry-gonnelly 1877 M. Church Hill 1877
15	Killesher	15	1798	Killesher 1855		
16	Kinawley	20	1761 Trinity (Holy) 1842	Kinawley 1835 Knockninny 1855		

NGA No.	CIVIL PARISH	GV No.	CHURCH OF IRELAND	ROMAN CATHOLIC	PRESBYTERIAN	OTHERS
17	Magheracross	9	1800	Irvinestown 1846		M. Ballina-mallard 1878
18	Magheraculmoney	4	1767	Magheraculmany (Ederny) 1836		
19	Rossory	8	1799	Enniskillen 1818		
20	Templecarn	3		Pettigo (Carn) 1836		
21	Tomregan	21	1797	Drumlane 1836 Kildallon 1867 Knockninny 1855		
22	Trory	10	1779	Irvinestown 1846		

NGA No.	CIVIL PARISH	GV No.	CHURCH OF IRELAND	ROMAN CATHOLIC	PRESBYTERIAN	OTHERS
1	Abbeygormacan	112		Abbeygormican & Killoran 1859		
2	Abbeyknockmoy	41		Abbeyknockmoy (No registers before 1880)		
3	Addergoole	10		Addergoole & Liskeevey 1858		
4	Ahascragh	78	1775	Ahascragh & Caltra 1840		
5	Annaghdown	36		Annaghdown 1834		
6	Ardrahan	66	1804	Ardrahan 1839		
7	Athenry	69	1796	Athenry 1858		
8	Athleague	49		Athleague & Fuerty 1808		
9	Aughrim	77	1814	Aughrim & Kilconnell 1828		
10	Ballindoon	4		Omey & Ballindoon 1838		
11	Ballymacward	46		Ballymacward & Clonkeenkerrill 1841		
12	Ballynacourty	56	1838	Kilcameen & Ballynacourty 1833		
13	Ballynakill	1, 19, 50, 105	1852	Ballynakill 1875 Kilbride 1853 Glinsk & Kilbegnet 1836 Moylough & Mountbellew 1848 Ballinakill 1839 Woodford 1821		
14	Beagh	90		Beagh 1849		
15	Belclare	30		Kilmoylan & Cummer 1813		
16	Boyounagh	18		Boyounagh & Templetoher 1838		
17	Bullaun	91		Bullaun, Grange & Killaan 1827		
18	Cargin	31		Killursa & Killower (No registers before 1880)		

47

NGA No.	CIVIL PARISH	GV No.	CHURCH OF IRELAND	ROMAN CATHOLIC	PRESBYTERIAN	OTHERS
19	Claregalway	55		Claregalway 1849		
20	Clonbern	22		Kilberrin & Clonberne 1855		
21	Clonfert	111		Clonfert, Donanaghta & Meelick 1829		
22	Clonkeen	45		Ballymacward & Clonkeenkerrill 1841		
23	Clontuskert	81	1821	Clontuskert 1827		
24	Cong	8		Cong & Neale 1870		
25	Cummer	34		Kilmoylan & Cummer 1813		
26	Donagh Patrick	26		Donaghpatrick & Kilcoona 1844		
27	Donanaghta	115		Clonfert, Donanaghta & Meelick 1829		
28	Drumacoo	62		Kilcolgan, Dromacoo & Killeenavara (Ballindereen) 1854		
29	Drumatemple	17		Oran (Cloverhill) 1845		
30	Duniry	103		Duniry & Kilnelahan 1839		
31	Dunmore	11		Dunmore 1833		
32	Fahy	114		Fahy & Kilquain 1836		
33	Fohanagh	71		Fohenagh & Kilgerrill 1827		
34	Grange	74		Bullaun, Grange & Killaan 1827		
35	Inishbofin	46 Mayo		Inisbofin 1867		
36	Inisheer	84		Aran Islands 1872		
37	Inishmaan	83		Aran Islands 1872		
38	Inishmore	82		Aran Islands 1872		

NGA No.	CIVIL PARISH	GV No.	CHURCH OF IRELAND	ROMAN CATHOLIC	PRESBYTERIAN	OTHERS
39	Isertkelly	93		Kilchreest 1855		
40	Kilbeacanty	89		Kilbeacanty 1854		
41	Kilbegnet	20		Glinsk & Kilbegnet 1836	Creggs 1863	
42	Kilbennan	13		Kilconly & Kilbannon 1872		
43	Kilchreest	95		Kilchreest 1855		
44	Kilcloony	80		Creagh & Kilclooney (St. Michael's) 1820	Ballinasloe	
45	Kilcolgan	63	1847	Kilcolgan, Dromacoo & Killeenavara (Ballindereen) 1854		
46	Kilconickny	68		Kilconickny, Kilconieran & Lickerrig 1831		
47	Kilconierin	61		Kilconickny, Kilconieran & Lickerrig 1831		
48	Kilconla	12		Kilconly & Kilbannon 1872		
49	Kilconnell	72		Aughrim & Kilconnell 1828		
50	Kilcooly	100		Kilcooley & Leitrim 1815		
51	Kilcoona	33		Donaghpatrick & Kilcoona 1844		
52	Kilcroan	16		Glinsk & Kilbegnet 1836		
53	Kilcummin	23	1812	Kilcummin (Oughterard) 1809 Rosmuck 1840 Lettermore 1848 Killeen 1853 Kilkerrin & Clonberne 1855		
54	Kilgerrill	79		Fohenagh & Kilgerrill 1827		
55	Kilkerrin	39		Kilkerrin & Clonberne 1855		

NGA No.	CIVIL PARISH	GV No.	CHURCH OF IRELAND	ROMAN CATHOLIC	PRESBYTERIAN	OTHERS
56	Kilkilvery	29		Killursa & Killower (No registers before 1880)		
57	Killaan	75		Bullaun, Grange & Killaan 1827		
58	Killallaghten	76		Killalaghteen & Kilrickill (Cappataggle) 1809		
59	Killannin	24	1844	Killannin 1875 Killeen 1853 Spiddal 1861		
60	Killeany	32		Killursa & Killower (No registers before 1880)		
61	Killeely	58		Kinvarra 1831		
62	Killeenadeema	96		Kilnadeema & Kilteskill 1836		
63	Killeenavarra	65		Kilcolgan, Dromacoo & Killeenavara (Ballindereen) 1854		
64	Killeenen	59		Killora & Killogilleen 1847		
65	Killererin	35		Killererin 1851		
66	Killeroran	48		Killian & Killeroran 1804		
67	Killian	47		Killian & Killeroran 1804		
68	Killimorbologue	116		Killimorbologue & Tiranascragh 1831		
69	Killimordaly	73		Killimordaly & Kiltullagh 1830		
70	Killinan	94		Kilchreest 1855		
71	Killinny	86		Kinvarra 1831 Kilmacduagh & Kiltartan (Gort) 1848		
72	Killogilleen	67		Killora & Kill-ogilleen 1847		

NGA No.	CIVIL PARISH	GV No.	CHURCH OF IRELAND	ROMAN CATHOLIC	PRESBYTERIAN	OTHERS
73	Killora	60		Killora & Killogilleen 1847		
74	Killoran	109		Abbeygormican & Killoran 1859		
75	Killoscobe	42		Killascobe 1807		
76	Killosolan	43		Ahascragh & Caltra 1840		
77	Killower	27		Killursa & Killower (No registers before 1880)		
78	Killursa	28		Killursa & Killower (No registers before 1880)		
79	Kilmacduagh	88		Kilmacduagh & Kiltartan (Gort) 1848		
80	Kilmalinoge	120		Kilmalinoge & Lickmolassy 1830		
81	Kilmeen	99		Kilmeen		
82	Kilmoylan	37	1855	Kilmoylan & Cummer 1813		
83	Kilquain	113		Fahy & Kilquain 1836		
84	Kilreekil	98		Killalaghten & Kilrickill (Cappataggle) 1809		
85	Kiltartan	87		Kilmacduagh & Kiltartan (Gort) 1848		
86	Kilteskil	101		Kilnadeema & Kilteskill 1836		
87	Kilthomas	97		Kilthomas 1854		
88	Kiltormer	110		Kiltormer & Oghill 1834		
89	Kiltullagh	70		Killimordaly & Kiltullagh 1830		
90	Kinvarradoorus	85		Kinvarra 1831		
91	Lackagh	38		Lackagh 1841		

NGA No.	CIVIL PARISH	GV No.	CHURCH OF IRELAND	ROMAN CATHOLIC	PRESBYTERIAN	OTHERS
92	Leitrim	102		Kilcooley & Leitrim 1815		
93	Lickerrig	64		Kilconickny, Kilconieran & Lickerrig 1831		
94	Lickmolassy	119	& Ballinakill Union 1766	Kilmalinoge & Lickmolassy 1830		
95	Liskeevy	9		Addergoole & Liskeevey 1858		
96	Loughrea	92	1747	Loughrea 1827		
97	Meelick	118		Clonfert, Donanaghta & Meelick 1829		
98	Monivea	44		Abbeyknockmoy (No registers before 1880) Athenry 1858		
99	Moycullen	25		Moycullen 1786 Spiddal 1861		
100	Moylough	40	1821	Moylough & Mountbellew 1848		
101	Moyrus	3	(Roundstone) 1841	Moyrus 1852 Roundstone 1872		
102	Omey	2	1831	Omey & Ballindoon 1838		
103	Oranmore	52		Kilcameen & Ballynacourty 1833		
104	Rahoon	53		Rahoon 1819 Salthill 1840		
105	Ross	7		Ross (Clonbur) 1853 Cong & Neale 1870		
106	St. Nicholas	54		St. Nicholas, Galway 1690 Castlegar 1827	Galway 1831	
107	Stradbally	57		Kilcornan 1837		
108	Taghboy	51		Dysert & Tissara 1850		
109	Templetogher	15		Boyounagh & Templetoher 1838		

NGA No.	CIVIL PARISH	GV No.	CHURCH OF IRELAND	ROMAN CATHOLIC	PRESBYTERIAN	OTHERS
110	Tiranascragh	117		Killimorbologue Tiranascragh 1831		
111	Tuam	14	1808	Tuam 1790		
112	Tynagh	104		Tynagh 1809		

COUNTY KERRY

NGA No.	CIVIL PARISH	GV No.	CHURCH OF IRELAND	ROMAN CATHOLIC	PRESBYTERIAN	OTHERS
1	Aghadoe	79	1842	Fossa 1857 Glenflesk 1821 Killorglin 1800 Killarney 1792		
2	Aghavallen	2	1845 marriages	Ballylongford 1823		
3	Aglish	75		Firies 1830		
4	Annagh	53		Ballymacelligott 1868 Tralee 1772		
5	Ardfert	25		Ardfert 1819 Spa 1866		
6	Ballincuslane	56		Brosna 1868 Castleisland 1822 Knocknagoshel 1850		
7	Ballinvoher	40		Annascaul 1829 Ballyferriter 1807		
8	Ballyconry	8		Ballybunion 1831		
9	Ballyduff	28		Castlegregory 1828		
10	Ballyheige	16		Ballyheigue 1857		
11	Ballymacelligott	49	1817	Ballymacelligott 1868		
12	Ballynacourty	39	1803	Annascaul 1829		
13	Ballynahaglish	45		Ardfert 1819 Spa 1866		
14	Ballyseedy	54	1830	Ballymacelligott 1868		
15	Brosna	52		Brosna 1868		
16	Caher	65		Cahirciveen 1846		
17	Castleisland	51	1835	Castleisland 1822 Knocknagoshel 1850 Brosna 1868		
18	Cloghane	27		Dingle 1821 Castlegregory 1828		
19	Clogherbrien	46		Ardfert 1819 Tralee 1772		

NGA No.	CIVIL PARISH	GV No.	CHURCH OF IRELAND	ROMAN CATHOLIC	PRESBYTERIAN	OTHERS
20	Currans	59		Ballymacelligott 1868 Killeentierna 1801		
21	Dingle	35	1707	Dingle 1821		
22	Dromod	70	& Prior 1827 marriages	Dromod 1850		
23	Duagh	15		Duagh 1819 Listowel 1802		
24	Dunquin	41		Ballyferriter 1807		
25	Dunurlin	32		Ballyferriter 1807		
26	Dysert	13, 61		Listowel 1802 Lixnaw 1810 Killeentierna 1801		
27	Fenit	44		Spa 1866		
28	Finuge	14		Listowel 1802 Lixnaw 1810		
29	Galey	6		Ballybunion 1831 Listowel 1802		
30	Garfinny	36		Dingle 1821		
31	Glanbehy	67		Glenbeigh 1830		
32	Kenmare	84	1799	Kenmare 1819 Tuosist 1844		
33	Kilbonane	74		Milltown 1821		
34	Kilcaragh	19		Lixnaw 1810		
35	Kilcaskan	87		Bonane 1846		
36	Kilcolman	62	1802	Milltown 1821		
37	Kilconly	1		Ballybunion 1831		
38	Kilcredane	76		Firies 1830		
39	Kilcrohane	82		Cahirdaniel 1831 Sneem 1845		
40	Kilcummin	77		Kilcummin 1821 Glenflesk 1821 Rathmore 1837		
41	Kildrum	43		Dingle 1821		
42	Kilfeighny	20		Abbeydorney 1835 Lixnaw 1810		

COUNTY KERRY

NGA No.	CIVIL PARISH	GV No.	CHURCH OF IRELAND	ROMAN CATHOLIC	PRESBYTERIAN	OTHERS
43	Kilflyn	24		Abbeydorney 1835		
44	Kilgarrylander	57		Castlemaine 1804		
45	Kilgarvan	85	1811	Kilgarvan 1818		
46	Kilgobban	31	1713	Annascaul 1829		
47	Killaha	81		Glenflesk 1821		
48	Killahan	17		Abbeydorney 1835		
49	Killarney	80		Killarney 1792 Glenflesk 1821	Killarney 1868	
50	Killeentierna	60		Killeentierna 1801		
51	Killehenny	4		Ballybunion 1831		
52	Killemlagh	68		Prior (Ballinskelligs) 1832		
53	Killinane	66		Cahirciveen 1846		
54	Killiney	30		Annascaul 1829 Castlegregory 1828		
55	Killorglin	63	1840	Killorglin 1800 Glenbeigh 1830		
56	Killury	11	& Rattoo 1867	Causeway 1782		
57	Kilmalkedar	34		Ballyferriter 1807		
58	Kilmoyly	22		Ardfert 1819		
59	Kilnanare	73		Firies 1830		
60	Kilnaughtin	3	1793	Tarbert 1859		
61	Kilquane	26		Ballyferriter 1807		
62	Kilshenane	21		Listowel 1802 Lixnaw 1810		
63	Kiltallagh	58		Castlemaine 1804		
64	Kiltomy	18		Abbeydorney 1835 Lixnaw 1810		
65	Kinard	37		Dingle 1821		
66	Knocknane	71		Killorglin 1800 Tuogh 1843		

NGA No.	CIVIL PARISH	GV No.	CHURCH OF IRELAND	ROMAN CATHOLIC	PRESBYTERIAN	OTHERS
67	Knockanure	10		Moyvane 1855		
68	Lisselton	5	1840	Ballybunion 1831		
69	Listowel	9	1790	Listowel 1802		
70	Marhin	33		Ballyferriter 1807		
71	Minard	38		Dingle 1821		
72	Molahiffe	72		Firies 1830		
73	Murhur	7		Moyvane 1855		
74	Nohaval	55		Ballymacelligott 1868		
75	Nohavaldaly	78		Boherbue 1833 Rathmore 1837		
76	O'Brennan	50		Ballymacelligott 1868		
77	O'Dorney	23		Abbeydorney 1835		
78	Prior	69	& Dromod 1827 marriages	Prior (Ballinskelligs) 1832		
79	Ratass	48	1850	Ballymacelligott 1868 Tralee 1772		
80	Rattoo	12	& Killury 1867	Causeway 1782		
81	Stradbally	29		Castlegregory 1828		
82	Templenoe	83		Kenmare 1819		
83	Tralee	47	1771	Tralee 1772	Tralee 1840	C. Tralee
84	Tuosist	86		Tuosist 1844		
85	Valencia	64	1826	Valentia 1825		
86	Ventry	42		Dingle 1821		

COUNTY KILDARE

NGA No.	CIVIL PARISH	GV No.	CHURCH OF IRELAND	ROMAN CATHOLIC	PRESBYTERIAN	OTHERS
1	Ardkill	10		Carbury 1821		
2	Ardree	104		Athy 1779		
3	Ballaghmoon	115		Castledermot 1789		
4	Ballybrackan	86		Monasterevin (Nurney) 1819		
5	Ballymany	63		Newbridge 1786		
6	Ballymore Eustace	77	1838	Ballymore Eustace 1779		
7	Ballynadrumny	1		Balyna (Johnstown) 1785		
8	Ballynafagh	30		Clane 1785		
9	Ballysax	64	1830	Newbridge 1786 Suncroft (Carragh) 1805		
10	Ballyshannon	92		Kildare & Rathangan 1815 Suncroft (Carragh) 1805 Narraghmore (Crookstown) 1827		
11	Balraheen	16		Clane 1785		
12	Belan	107		Castledermot 1789		
13	Bodenstown	36		Kill 1840		
14	Brannockstown	78		Kilcullen 1777		
15	Brideschurch	35		Caragh (Downings) 1849		
16	Cadamstown	4		Balyna (Johnstown) 1785		
17	Carbury	9	Castlecarbery 1814	Carbury 1821 Balyna (Johnstown) 1785		
18	Carn	65		Suncroft (Carragh) 1805		
19	Carnalway	75	1846 marriages	Newbridge 1786		
20	Carragh	34		Caragh (Downings) 1849		
21	Carrick	5		Balyna (Johnstown) 1785		
22	Castledermot	111		Castledermot 1789		
23	Castledillon	46		Celbridge 1857		

58

NGA No.	CIVIL PARISH	GV No.	CHURCH OF IRELAND	ROMAN CATHOLIC	PRESBYTERIAN	OTHERS
24	Churchtown	96	Athy 1669	Athy 1779	Athy	Q. Athy
25	Clane	33	1802	Clane 1785		
26	Clonaghlis	48		Celbridge 1857		
27	Cloncurry	12, 56		Kilcock 1770 Kildare & Rathangan 1815		
28	Clonshanbo	15		Kilcock 1770		
29	Confey	21		Maynooth & Leixlip 1806		
30	Davidstown	99		Narraghmore (Crookstown) 1827		
31	Donadea	18		Clane 1785		
32	Donaghcumper	44		Celbridge 1857		
33	Donaghmore	22	1720	Maynooth & Leixlip 1806		
34	Downings	31		Caragh (Downings) 1849		
35	Duneany	84		Monasterevin (Nurney) 1819		
36	Dunfierth	7		Carbury 1821		
37	Dunmanoge	110		Castledermot 1789		
38	Dunmurraghill	17		Clane 1785		
39	Dunmurry	59		Kildare & Rathangan 1815		
40	Feighcullen	68		Allen (Kilmeague) 1820		
41	Fontstown	93		Narraghmore (Crookstown) 1827		
42	Forenaghts	52		Kill 1840		
43	Gilltown	79		Kilcullen 1777		
44	Graney	113		Baltinglass 1807 Castledermot 1789		
45	Grangeclare	58		Kildare & Rathangan 1815		
46	Grangerosnolvan	106		Castledermot 1789		
47	Greatconnell	72		Newbridge 1786		

NGA No.	CIVIL PARISH	GV No.	CHURCH OF IRELAND	ROMAN CATHOLIC	PRESBYTERIAN	OTHERS
48	Harristown	89	1666	Monasterevin (Nurney) 1819		
49	Haynestown	53		Kill 1840		
50	Johnstown	41		Kill 1840		
51	Kerdiffstown	39		Kill 1840		
52	Kilberry	95		Athy 1779		
53	Kilcock	13		Kilcock 1770		
54	Kilcullen	94	1778	Kilcullen 1777		
55	Kildangan	87		Monasterevin (Nurney) 1819		
56	Kildare	61	1801	Kildare & Rathangan 1815 Curragh Camp 1855		
57	Kildrought	26	or Celbridge 1777	Celbridge 1857		
58	Kilkea	109		Castledermot 1789		
59	Kill	50	1814	Kill 1840 Newbridge 1786		
60	Killadoon	27		Celbridge 1857		
61	Killashee	73		Newbridge 1786		
62	Killelan	108		Castledermot 1789		
63	Killybegs	32		Caragh (Downings) 1849		
64	Kilmacredock	23		Maynooth & Leixlip 1806		
65	Kilmeage	66		Allen (Kilmeague) 1820		
66	Kilmore	8		Carbury 1821		
67	Kilpatrick	11		Clonbullogue 1808		
68	Kilrainy	2		Balyna (Johnstown) 1785		
69	Kilrush	91		Suncroft (Carragh) 1805		
70	Kilteel	51		Blessington 1852		
71	Kineagh	112		Castledermot 1789		

NGA No.	CIVIL PARISH	GV No.	CHURCH OF IRELAND	ROMAN CATHOLIC	PRESBYTERIAN	OTHERS
72	Knavinstown	83		Kildare & Rathangan 1815		
73	Lackagh	82	1830	Kildare & Rathangan 1815 Monasterevin (Nurney) 1819		
74	Ladytown	71		Caragh (Downings) 1849		
75	Laraghbryan	20		Maynooth & Leixlip 1806		
76	Leixlip	24	1669	Maynooth & Leixlip 1806		
77	Lullymore	54		Kildare & Rathangan 1815		
78	Lyons	47		Celbridge 1857		
79	Mainham	19		Clane 1785		
80	Monasterevin	85		Monasterevin (Nurney) 1819		
81	Moone	103		Kildare & Rathangan 1815 Castledermot 1789		
82	Morristownbiller	69		Newbridge 1786		
83	Mylerstown	3		Balyna (Johnstown) 1785		
84	Naas	40	1679	Naas 1813	Naas 1857	
85	Narraghmore	101		Narraghmore (Crookstown) 1827		
86	Nurney	6, 90		Balyna (Johnstown) 1785 Monasterevin (Nurney) 1819		
87	Oldconnell	70		Newbridge 1786		
88	Oughterard	49		Kill 1840		
89	Painestown	114		Carlow 1769		
90	Pollardstown	62		Allen (Kilmeague) 1820		
91	Rathangan	55		Kildare & Rathangan 1815		
92	Rathernan	67		Allen (Kilmeague) 1820		
93	Rathmore	43		Blessington 1852		

NGA No.	CIVIL PARISH	GV No.	CHURCH OF IRELAND	ROMAN CATHOLIC	PRESBYTERIAN	OTHERS
94	St. John's	98		Athy 1779		
95	St. Michael's	97		Athy 1779		
96	Scullogestown	14		Kilcock 1770		
97	Sherlockstown	38		Kill 1840		
98	Stacumny	45		Celbridge 1857		
99	Straffan	28	1838	Celbridge 1857		
100	Taghadoe	25		Maynooth & Leixlip 1806		
101	Tankardstown	105		Athy 1779		
102	Thomastown	57		Kildare & Rathangan 1815		
103	Timahoe	29		Clane 1785		
104	Timolin	102	1812	Castledermot 1789		
105	Tipper	42		Naas 1813		
106	Tipperkevin	74		Ballymore Eustace 1779		
107	Tully	60		Kildare & Rathangan 1815		
108	Usk	100		Narraghmore (Crookstown) 1827		
109	Walterstown	88		Monasterevin (Nurney) 1819		
110	Whitechurch	37		Kill 1840		

NGA No.	CIVIL PARISH	GV No.	CHURCH OF IRELAND	ROMAN CATHOLIC	PRESBYTERIAN	OTHERS
1	Abbeyleix	14		Abbeyleix 1824		
2	Aghaviller	104		Aghaviller 1847		
3	Aglish	140		Mooncoin 1772 Slieverue 1766		
4	Aharney	10		Ballyragget 1856 Lisdowney 1771		
5	Arderra	136		Mooncoin 1772		
6	Attanagh	13		Ballyragget 1856		
7	Balleen	7		Lisdowney 1771		
8	Ballinamara	38		Freshford 1773 Tullaroan 1843		
9	Ballybur	52		Danesfort 1819		
10	Ballycallan	41		Kilmanagh 1845		
11	Ballygurrim	119		Glenmore 1831		
12	Ballylarkin	32		Freshford 1773 Urlingford 1805		
13	Ballylinch	83		Thomastown 1782		
14	Ballytarsney	135		Mooncoin 1772		
15	Ballytobin	97		Dunnamaggan 1826		
16	Blackrath	66	1810	Claragh 1855		
17	Blanchvilleskill	74		Claragh 1855 Gowran 1809		
18	Borrismore	6		Urlingford 1805		
19	Burnchurch	56		Danesfort 1819		
20	Callan	47		Callan 1821		
21	Castlecomer	15	1799 Castlecomer Colliery 1838	Castlecomer 1812 Clough 1858 Muckalee 1801		
22	Castleinch or Inchyolaghan	51		St. Patrick's, Kilkenny 1800		
23	Clara	70		Claragh 1855		
24	Clashacrow	36		Freshford 1773		
25	Clomantagh	28		Freshford 1773 Urlingford 1805		
26	Clonamery	112		Inistiogue 1810		
27	Clonmore	131	1817	Mooncoin 1772		

COUNTY KILKENNY

NGA No.	CIVIL PARISH	GV No.	CHURCH OF IRELAND	ROMAN CATHOLIC	PRESBYTERIAN	OTHERS
28	Columbkille	89		Thomastown 1782		
29	Coolaghmore	93		Windgap 1822		
30	Coolcashin	8		Lisdowney 1771		
31	Coolcraheen	22		Conahy 1832 Lisdowney 1771		
32	Danesfort	57		Danesfort 1819		
33	Derrynahinch	106		Ballyhale 1823		
34	Donaghmore	18		Ballyragget 1856		
35	Dunbell	73		Claragh 1855		
36	Dungarvan	81		Gowran 1809		
37	Dunkitt	121	1753	Kilmacow 1858 Mullinavat 1843 Slieverue 1766		
38	Dunmore	26	1857 marriages	St. John's, Kilkenny 1809		
39	Dunnamaggan	98		Dunnamaggan 1826 Aghaviller 1847		
40	Durrow	11		Durrow 1789 Ballyragget 1856		
41	Dysart	21		Castlecomer 1812 Muckalee 1801		
42	Dysartmoon	113		Rosbercon 1817		
43	Earlstown	59		Callan 1821		
44	Ennisnag	60		Aghaviller 1847 Danesfort 1819		
45	Erke	1		Galmoy 1861 Johnstown 1814		
46	Famma	91		Thomastown 1814		
47	Fertagh	4	1797	Johnstown 1814		
48	Fiddown	128	(Rathkearan) 1686	Mooncoin 1772 Templeorum 1803		
49	Freshford	33		Freshford 1773		
50	Garranamanagh	29		Freshford 1773		
51	Gaulskill	122	Dunkitt 1753	Kilmacow 1858 Mullinavat 1853		
52	Glashare	2		Galmoy 1861 Lisdowney 1771		

NGA No.	CIVIL PARISH	GV No.	CHURCH OF IRELAND		ROMAN CATHOLIC	PRESBYTERIAN	OTHERS
53	Gowran	71			Gowran 1809		
54	Graiguenamanagh	86	Graigue 1827		Graiguenamanagh 1818		
55	Grange	50			Danesfort 1819		
56	Grangekilree	58			Danesfort 1819		
57	Grangemaccomb	19			Ballyragget 1856 Conahy 1832 Lisdowney 1771		
58	Grangesilvia	76	1850 marriages		Paulstown 1824		
59	Inistioge	92	1797		Inistiogue 1810 Thomastown 1782		
60	Jerpointabbey	88			Thomastown 1782		
61	Jerpointchurch	102			Aghaviller 1847 Ballyhale 1823 Thomastown 1782		
62	Jerpointwest	108			Rosbercon 1817 Thomastown 1782		
63	Kells	95			Danesfort 1819 Dunnamaggan 1826		
64	Kilbeacon	110	1813		Mullinavat 1843		
65	Kilbride	117			Glenmore 1831		
66	Kilcoan	118			Glenmore 1831		
67	Kilcolumb	123	1817 Dunkitt 1753		Glenmore 1831 Slieverue 1766		
68	Kilcooly	34			Urlingford 1805		
69	Kilculliheen	13 Waterford		Macully 1817	Slieverue 1766		
70	Kilderry	67			St. John's, Kilkenny 1809		
71	Kilfane	85			Thomastown 1782 Tullaherin 1782		
72	Kilferagh	54			St. Patrick's, Kilkenny 1800		
73	Kilkeasy	105			Aghaviller 1847 Ballyhale 1823		
74	Kilkieran	63			St. John's, Kilkenny 1809		
75	Killahy	35, 109			Urlingford 1805 Mullinavat 1843		
76	Killaloe	48			Callan 1821 Kilmanagh 1845		

NGA No.	CIVIL PARISH	GV No.	CHURCH OF IRELAND	ROMAN CATHOLIC	PRESBYTERIAN	OTHERS
77	Killamery	96		Callan 1821 Windgap 1822		
78	Killarney	79		Tullaherin 1782		
79	Kilmacahill	72		Paulstown 1824		
80	Kilmacar	20		Ballyragget 1856 Castlecomer 1812 Conahy 1832		
81	Kilmacnow	138	1792	Kilmacow 1858		
82	Kilmademoge	27		Muckalee 1801		
83	Kilmadum	62		Muckalee 1801		
84	Kilmaganny	100	1782	Aghaviller 1847 Dunnamaggan 1826 Windgap 1822		
85	Kilmakevoge	124		Glenmore 1831		
86	Kilmanagh	40	1784	Kilmanagh 1845		
87	Kilmenan	17		Ballyragget 1856		
88	Kilree	99		Dunnamaggan 1826		
89	Knocktopher	103		Aghaviller 1847 Ballyhale 1823 Thomastown 1782		
90	Lismateige	107		Aghaviller 1847		
91	Listerlin	115		Rosbercon 1817		
92	Mallardstown	94		Callan 1821		
93	Mayne	23		Conahy 1832 Muckalee 1801		
94	Mothell	24		Muckalee 1801		
95	Muckalee	25, 130		Muckalee 1801 Mooncoin 1772 Mullinavat 1843 Templeorum 1803		
96	Odagh	39		Conahy 1832 Freshford 1773		
97	Outrath	53		St. Patrick's, Kilkenny 1800		
98	Owning	127		Templeorum 1803		
99	Pleberstown	90		Thomastown 1782		
100	Pollrone	134		Mooncoin 1772		

COUNTY KILKENNY

NGA No.	CIVIL PARISH	GV No.	CHURCH OF IRELAND	ROMAN CATHOLIC	PRESBYTERIAN	OTHERS
101	Portnascully	139		Mooncoin 1772		
102	Powerstown	82		Graiguenamanagh 1818		
103	Rathaspick	16		Clough 1858		
104	Rathbeagh	30		Ballyragget 1856 Lisdowney 1771		
105	Rathcoole	64		Muckalee 1801 St. John's, Kilkenny 1809		
106	Rathkieran	133	Fiddown (Rathkearan) 1686	Mooncoin 1772 Mullinavat 1843		
107	Rathlogan	5		Johnstown 1814		
108	Rathpatrick	125	Macully 1817	Slieverue 1766		
109	Rosbercon	116		Rosbercon 1817		
110	Rosconnell	12		Ballyragget 1856		
111	Rossinan	111		Mullinavat 1843		
112	St. Canice's	42	Kilkenny 1789	St. Canice's, Kilkenny 1768 St. Patrick's, Kilkenny 1800		
113	St. John's	43		St. John's, Kilkenny 1809		
114	St. Martin's	69		Claragh 1855		
115	St. Mary's	44	Kilkenny 1729	St. Mary's, Kilkenny 1754	Kilkenny	M. Kilkenny Q. Kilkenny
116	St. Maul's	45		St. Canice's Kilkenny 1768		
117	St. Patrick's	46		St. Patrick's, Kilkenny 1800		
118	Shanbogh	120		Rosbercon 1817		
119	Shankill	68		Paulstown 1824		
120	Sheffin	9		Lisdowney 1771		
121	Stonecarthy	61		Aghaviller 1847		
122	The Rower	114		Inistiogue 1810		
123	Thomastown	84		Thomastown 1782		
124	Tibberaghny	129		Templeorum 1803		
125	Tiscoffin	65		Claragh 1855		
126	Treadingstown	77		Tullaherin 1782		

NGA No.	CIVIL PARISH	GV No.	CHURCH OF IRELAND	ROMAN CATHOLIC	PRESBYTERIAN	OTHERS
127	Tubbrid	132		Mooncoin 1772		
128	Tubbridbritain	31		Freshford 1773 Urlingford 1805		
129	Tullaghanbrogue	49		Danesfort 1819 Kilmanagh 1845		
130	Tullaherin	80		Tullaherin 1782		
131	Tullahought	101		Windgap 1822		
132	Tullamaine	55		Callan 1821		
133	Tullaroan	37		Tullaroan 1843		
134	Ullard	87		Graiguenamanagh 1818		
135	Ullid	137		Kilmacow 1858		
136	Urlingford	3		Urlingford 1805		
137	Wells	75		Paulstown 1824		
138	Whitechurch	120	or Castlane 1846 marriages	Templeorum 1803		
139	Woolengrange	78		Thomastown 1782 Tullaherin 1782		

NGA No.	CIVIL PARISH	GV No.	CHURCH OF IRELAND	ROMAN CATHOLIC	PRESBYTERIAN	OTHERS
1	Annaduff	13		Annaduff 1849		
2	Carrigallen	15		Carrigallen 1829	Carrigallen 1861 (united with Belturbet 1919 & with Killashandra 1930)	
3	Cloonclare	5	or Manorhamilton 1816	Cloonclare 1841		M. Manorhamilton
4	Cloone	17		Cloone–Conmaicne 1820 Aghavas 1845 Gortletheragh 1826		
5	Cloonlogher	4		Drumlease 1859 Killargue 1852		
6	Drumlease	3	1828	Drumlease 1859		
7	Drumreilly	9		Drumreilly 1867		
8	Fenagh	12		Fenagh 1825		
9	Inishmagrath	8		Inishmagrath 1835	Drumkeeran 1835 (united with Carrigallen 1881)	
10	Killanummery	6		Killenummery & Killerry 1827	Creevelea 1852	
11	Killarga	7		Killargue 1852		
12	Killasnet	2		Killasnet 1852		
13	Kiltoghert	10	1810	Kiltoghert 1826 Murhan (Drum-shambo) 1861 Bornacoola 1836		
14	Kiltubbrid	11		Kiltubbrid 1841		
15	Mohill	16	1785	Mohil–Manachain 1836		
16	Oughteragh	14	1833	Oughteragh 1869		
17	Rossinver	1		Rossinver 1844 Kinlough 1835 Glenade 1867		

NGA No.	CIVIL PARISH	GV No.	CHURCH OF IRELAND	ROMAN CATHOLIC	PRESBYTERIAN	OTHERS
1	Abbeyleix	41	1781	Abbeyleix 1824 Ballyragget 1856		B. Abbeyleix
2	Aghaboe	23		Aghaboe 1794 Borris-in-Ossory 1840	Ballacolla 1858 (united with Mountmellick 1926)	
3	Aghmacart	32		Durrow 1829		
4	Aharney	36		Ballyragget 1856 Lisdowney 1771		
5	Ardea	5	Mountmellick 1840	Mountmellick 1814	Mountmellick 1849	Q. Mountmellick
6	Attanagh	37		Ballyragget 1856		
7	Ballyadams	43		Ballyadams 1820		
8	Ballyroan	38		Abbeyleix 1824		
9	Bordwell	29		Aghaboe 1794		
10	Borris	10	Maryborough 1793	Portlaoise 1826		M. Maryborough
11	Castlebrack	1		Mountmellick 1814 Rosenallis 1765		
12	Clonenagh & Clonagheen	9	1749 Ballyfinn 1821	Ballyfin 1819 Mountrath 1823 Raheen 1819		Q. Mountrath
13	Cloydagh	53		Leighlinbridge 1783		
14	Coolbanagher	6	1802	Emo 1875 Mountmellick 1814		
15	Coolkerry	31		Aghaboe 1794 Rathdowney 1763		
16	Curraclone	18		Stradbally 1820		
17	Donaghmore	25		Rathdowney 1763		
18	Durrow	33	1731	Durrow 1829 Ballyragget 1856		
19	Dysartenos	14		Portlaoise 1826		
20	Dysartgallen	42		Ballinakill 1794		
21	Erke	27		Galmoy 1861		
22	Fossy or Timahoe	40	1845	Stradbally 1820		
23	Glashare	35		Lisdowney 1771		

COUNTY LEIX (QUEEN'S COUNTY)

NGA No.	CIVIL PARISH	GV No.	CHURCH OF IRELAND	ROMAN CATHOLIC	PRESBYTERIAN	OTHERS
24	Kilcolmanbane	13		Portlaoise 1826		
25	Kilcolmanbrack	39		Stradbally 1820		
26	Kildellig	28		Aghaboe 1794		
27	Killabban	49	(Castletown) 1802	Arles 1821 Doonane 1843		
28	Killenny	15		Portlaoise 1826		
29	Killermogh	30		Aghaboe 1794		
30	Killeshin	51	1824	Graigue 1819		
31	Kilmanman	2		Clonaslee 1849		
32	Kilteale	12		Portlaoise 1826		
33	Kyle	21		Roscrea & Corbally 1810		
34	Lea	7	1801 St. Paul's, Portarlington 1694	Portarlington 1820		
35	Monksgrange	48		Arles 1821		
36	Moyanna	16		Stradbally 1820		
37	Offerlane	8	1807	Borris-in-Ossory 1840 Camross 1820 Castletown 1772		
38	Rathaspick	47		Ballyadams 1820		
39	Rathdowney	24	1756	Rathdowney 1763		
40	Rathsaran	26	1810	Rathdowney 1763		
41	Rearymore	3		Rosenallis 1765		
42	Rosconnell	34		Ballyragget 1856		
43	Rosenallis	4	Oregan 1801 Mountmellick 1840	Mountmellick 1814 Rosenallis 1765	Mountmellick 1849	Q. Mountmellick
44	St. John's	44		Athy 1779		
45	Shrule	50		Arles 1821		
46	Skirk	22		Borris-in-Ossory 1840 Rathdowney 1763		
47	Sleaty	52		Graigue 1819		
48	Straboe	11		Portlaoise 1826		
49	Stradbally	17	1772	Stradbally 1820		
50	Tankardstown	46		Athy 1779		

NGA No.	CIVIL PARISH	GV No.	CHURCH OF IRELAND	ROMAN CATHOLIC	PRESBYTERIAN	OTHERS
51	Tecolm	45		Ballyadams 1820		
52	Timogue	19		Stradbally 1820		
53	Tullomoy	20		Ballyadams 1820		

NGA No.	CIVIL PARISH	GV No.	CHURCH OF IRELAND	ROMAN CATHOLIC	PRESBYTERIAN	OTHERS
1	Abbeyfeale	74		Abbeyfeale 1856		
2	Abington	61	1811	Munroe & Boher 1814		
3	Adare	89	1804	Adare 1832		
4	Aglishcormick	60		Kilteely 1815		
5	Anhid	93		Croom 1770		
6	Ardagh	11	& Rathronan 1818	Ardagh 1841		
7	Ardcanny	27	1802	Kildimo 1831		
8	Ardpatrick	121		Ardpatrick 1861 Kilfinane 1832		
9	Askeaton	14		Askeaton 1829		
10	Athlacca	95		Dromin 1817		
11	Athneasy	116		Bulgaden & Ballinvana 1812		
12	Ballinard	109		Hospital 1810		
13	Ballingaddy	122		Kilmallock 1837		
14	Ballingarry	81, 125	1785	Ballingarry 1825 Banogue 1861 Ballylanders 1849		
15	Ballinlough	111		Hospital 1810		
16	Ballybrood	57		Caherconlish 1841		
17	Ballycahane	38		Fedamore 1806		
18	Ballylanders	126		Ballylanders 1849		
19	Ballynaclogh	66		Pallasgreen 1811		
20	Ballynamona	110		Hospital 1810		
21	Ballyscaddan	119		Emly 1809		
22	Bruff	96	1850	Bruff 1808		
23	Bruree	84		Rockhill 1842		
24	Caheravally	50		Donaghmore 1827		
25	Caherconlish	53		Caherconlish 1841		
26	Cahercorney	106		Hospital 1810		
27	Caherelly	55		Ballybricken 1800		

NGA No.	CIVIL PARISH	GV No.	CHURCH OF IRELAND	ROMAN CATHOLIC	PRESBYTERIAN	OTHERS
28	Cahernarry	51	1857	Donaghmore 1827		
29	Cappagh	17		Cappagh 1841 Stonehall 1825		
30	Carrigparson	49		Ballybricken 1800 Caherconlish 1841		
31	Castletown	64		Doon 1824		
32	Chapelrussell	26	1822	Kildimo 1831		
33	Clonagh	19		Coolcappa or Kilcolman 1827		
34	Cloncagh	80		Knockaderry 1838		
35	Cloncrew	86		Drumcollogher 1830		
36	Clonelty	73		Knockaderry 1838		
37	Clonkeen	47		Murroe & Boher 1814		
38	Clonshire	18		Adare 1832 Cappagh 1841		
39	Colmanswell	87		Ballyagran & Colmanswell 1841		
40	Corcomohide	83	1805	Ballyagran & Colmanswell 1841		
41	Crecora	35		Mungret 1844 Patrick's Well 1801		
42	Croagh	22		Croagh 1836 Cappagh 1841		
43	Croom	91		Croom 1770 Banogue 1861 Manistir 1826		
44	Darragh	129		Glenroe 1853		
45	Derrygalvin	46		St. Patrick's, Limerick 1812		
46	Donaghmore	48		Donaghmore 1827		
47	Doon	63	1804	Doon 1824 Cappamore 1843 Murroe & Boher 1814		
48	Doondonnell	20		Coolcappa or Kilcolman 1827		

NGA No.	CIVIL PARISH	GV No.	CHURCH OF IRELAND	ROMAN CATHOLIC	PRESBYTERIAN	OTHERS
49	Drehidtarsna	90		Adare 1832		
50	Dromin	97		Dromin 1817 Bruff 1808		
51	Dromkeen	58		Caherconlish 1841 Kilteely 1815 Pallasgreen 1811		
52	Dromcolliher	85		Drumcollogher 1830		
53	Dunmoylan	7		Coolcappa or Kilcolman 1827		
54	Dysert	92		Croom 1770		
55	Effin	102		Effin 1843		
56	Emlygreennan	117		Bulgaden & Ballinvana 1812		
57	Fedamore	104	1840	Fedamore 1806		
58	Galbally	120		Galbally 1809		
59	Glenogra	105		Bruff 1808 Fedamore 1806		
60	Grange	72		Knockaderry 1838		
61	Grean	65		Kilteely 1815 Pallasgreen 1811		
62	Hackmys	100		Charleville 1774		
63	Hospital	112		Hospital 1810		
64	Inch St. Lawrence	56		Caherconlish 1841		
65	Iveruss	24		Askeaton 1829		
66	Kilbeheny	130		Kilbehenny 1824		
67	Kilbolane	88		Freemount 1827		
68	Kilbradran	9		Coolcappa or Kilcolman 1827		
69	Kilbreedy-Major	115		Ardpatrick 1861 Bulgaden & Ballinvana 1812		
70	Kilbreedy-Minor	101		Effin 1843		
71	Kilcolman	8		Coolcappa or Kilcolman 1827		
72	Kilcornan	25		Stonehall 1825		

NGA No.	CIVIL PARISH	GV No.	CHURCH OF IRELAND	ROMAN CATHOLIC	PRESBYTERIAN	OTHERS
73	Kilcullane	108		Hospital 1810		
74	Kildimo	28	1809	Kildimo 1831		
75	Kilfergus	2	& Kilmoylan 1812	Glin 1851		
76	Kilfinnane	124	1804	Kilfinane 1832		
77	Kilfinny	79		Croagh 1836		
78	Kilflyn	128	1813	Glenroe 1853		
79	Kilfrush	113		Hospital 1810		
80	Kilkeedy	29	1799	Kildimo 1831 Mungret 1844		
81	Killagholehane	78		Drumcollogher 1830		
82	Killeedy	77		Killeedy 1840 Monagea 1777 Newcastle West 1815 Tournafulla 1867		
83	Killeely	30		St. Munchin's, Limerick 1764		
84	Killeenagarriff	43		Castleconnell 1850		
85	Killeenoghty	37		Patrick's Well 1801		
86	Killonahan	34		Patrick's Well 1801		
87	Kilmeedy	82	Corcomohide 1805	Ballyagran & Colmanswell 1841 Feenagh 1854		
88	Kilmoylan	6	& Kilfergus 1812	Shanagolden 1824		
89	Kilmurry	42		Parteen 1814 St. Patrick's, Limerick 1812		
90	Kilpeacon	103		Fedamore 1806 Mungret 1844 Patrick's Well 1801		
91	Kilquane	127		Kilmallock 1837		
92	Kilscannell	23	& Rathkeale 1746	Ardagh 1841 Rathkeale 1811		
93	Kilteely	69		Kilteely 1815		
94	Knockainy	107	Aney 1760	Knockaney 1808		

NGA No.	CIVIL PARISH	GV No.	CHURCH OF IRELAND	ROMAN CATHOLIC	PRESBYTERIAN	OTHERS
95	Knocklong	118		Knocklong 1809		
96	Knocknagaul	36		Mungret 1844		
	Limerick City					
97	St. John's	1	1697	St. John's 1788 St. Mary's 1745		
98	St. Lawrence's	44	(Trinity Church) 1863	St. Patrick's 1812		
99	St. Mary's	1	1726	St. Mary's 1745		
100	St. Michael's	33	1801	St. Michael's 1772	Limerick 1829	M. Limerick C. Limerick B. Limerick Q. Limerick
101	St. Munchin's	31	1700	St. Munchin's 1764 St. Mary's 1745		
102	St. Nicholas'	45		St. Mary's 1745 St. Munchin's 1764		
103	St. Patrick's	41		St. Patrick's 1812 Parteen 1814		
104	Lismakeery	15		Askeaton 1829		
105	Loghill	3		Loughill 1855		
106	Ludden	52		Ballybricken 1800		
107	Mahoonagh	76		Mahoonagh 1810		
108	Monagay	75		Monagea 1777 Newcastle West 1815 Templeglantine 1864		
109	Monasteranenagh	39		Bruff 1808 Fedamore 1806 Manistir 1826		
110	Morgans	12		Shanagolden 1824		
111	Mungret	32		Mungret 1844		
112	Nantinan	16		Stonehall 1825		
113	Newcastle	71	1848	Newcastle West 1815		
114	Oola	68		Oola & Solohead 1809		
115	Particles	123	(With Kilflyn) 1841	Kilfinane 1832		

COUNTY LIMERICK

NGA No.	CIVIL PARISH	GV No.	CHURCH OF IRELAND	ROMAN CATHOLIC	PRESBYTERIAN	OTHERS
116	Rathjordan	59		Hospital 1810		
117	Rathkeale	21	1742 & Kilscannell 1746	Rathkeale 1811		
118	Rathronan	10	& Ardagh 1818	Ardagh 1841 Athea 1827		
119	Robertstown	5		Shanagolden 1824		
120	Rochestown	54		Ballybricken 1800		
121	St. Peter's & St. Paul's	114		Kilmallock 1837		
122	Shanagolden	4	1803	Shanagolden 1824		
123	Stradbally	40	1787	Castleconnell 1850		
124	Tankardstown	99		Kilmallock 1837		
125	Templebredon	70		Pallasgreen 1811		
126	Tomdeely	13		Askeaton 1829		
127	Tullabracky	94	1820	Bruff 1808		
128	Tuogh	62	& Cappamore 1858	Cappamore 1843		
129	Tuoghcluggin	67		Oola & Solohead 1809		
130	Uregare	98		Bruff 1808 Dromin 1817		

NGA No.	CIVIL PARISH	GV No.	CHURCH OF IRELAND	ROMAN CATHOLIC	PRESBYTERIAN	OTHERS
1	Aghadowey	20		Coleraine 1843	Aghadowey 1851 Ballylintagh 1872 (Church dissolved 1883) Ringsend	
2	Aghanloo	8		Magilligan 1863 Limavady 1855		
3	Agivey	21		Coleraine 1843		
4	Arboe	46	1773	Arboe 1827		
5	Artrea	42	1811 Ballyeglish 1868 Woods Chapel 1800	Moneymore 1830	Moneymore 1827 Saltersland 1847	
6	Ballinderry	48	1802	Ballinderry 1826		
7	Ballyaghran	2		Coleraine 1843	Portstewart 1829	
8	Ballymoney	6	1807	Ballymoney 1853		
9	Ballynascreen	36	1808	Ballynascreen 1825	Draperstown 1837	
10	Ballyrashane	4		Coleraine 1843	Ballyrashane 1863 Ballywatt 1867	
11	Ballyscullion	39		Ballyscullion 1844 Magherafelt 1834	Bellaghy	
12	Ballywillin	1	1826	Coleraine 1843	Portrush 1843 Ballywillin 1840	
13	Balteagh	12		Limavady 1855	Balteagh 1868	
14	Banagher	15	(Feeny) 1821	Banagher 1848 Dungiven 1847	Banagher 1834	
15	Bovevagh	13		Banagher 1848 Dungiven 1847 Limavady 1855	Bovevagh 1818	
16	Carrick	11		Limavady 1855	Largy 1848	
17	Clondermot	27	1810 Clooney 1867	Glendermot (Waterside) 1864	1st & 2nd Glendermot 1855 (united 1910) Gortnessy 1839 Waterside 1866	R.P. Faughan
18	Coleraine	3	1769	Coleraine 1843	Coleraine – 1st 1845 2nd or New Row 1842 3rd or Terrace Row 1845	M. Coleraine 1831 C. Coleraine 1837 B. Coleraine

COUNTY LONDONDERRY

NGA No.	CIVIL PARISH	GV No.	CHURCH OF IRELAND	ROMAN CATHOLIC	PRESBYTERIAN	OTHERS
19	Cumber Lower	28	1804	Cumber Upper 1863 Glendermot 1864	Cumber Lower 1827	
20	Cumber Upper	30	1811	Banagher 1848 Cumber Upper 1863	Cumber Upper 1834	
21	Derryloran	45	1796	Desertcreight 1827		
22	Desertlyn	44	1797	Magherafelt 1834 Moneymore 1830		
23	Desertmartin	40	1785	Desertmartin 1848	Lecumpher 1825	
24	Desertoghill	23		Errigal 1846 Kilrea 1846	Moneydig 1857	
25	Drumachose	10	1728	Limavady 1855	Limavady – 1st 1832 2nd 1845 Drumachose 1838 Derramore 1825	R.P. Limavady M. Limavady 1841 C. Limavady
26	Dunboe	16	1822 Castlerock 1870	Coleraine 1843 Magilligan 1863	Dunboe – 1st 1843 2nd 1864	
27	Dungiven	14	1778	Dungiven 1847	Dungiven 1835 Scriggan	
28	Errigal	22		Errigal 1846	Garvagh – 1st 1795 2nd 1830 3rd (dissolved 1908)	R.P. Garvagh
29	Faughanvale	26	1802	Faughanvale 1860	Faughanvale 1819	
30	Formoyle	18	1860	Magilligan 1863		
31	Kilcronaghan	37	1749	Desertmartin 1848	Tobermore	
32	Kildollagh	5		Coleraine 1843		
33	Killelagh	33		Maghera 1841		
34	Killowen	17	1824	Coleraine 1843		
35	Kilrea	32	1801	Kilrea 1846	Kilrea – 1st 1825 2nd 1840	
36	Learmount	31	1832	Banagher 1848		
37	Lissan	43	1753	Lissan 1839		
38	Macosquin	19		Coleraine 1843	Crossgar 1839 Killaig 1805 Macosquin	

COUNTY LONDONDERRY

NGA No.	CIVIL PARISH	GV No.	CHURCH OF IRELAND	ROMAN CATHOLIC	PRESBYTERIAN	OTHERS
39	Maghera	34	1785	Maghera 1841	Maghera 1843 Curran 1840 Swatragh	S.P. Culnady S.P. Knock- loughrim M. Maghera 1825
40	Magherafelt	41	1718 Castledawson 1844	Magherafelt 1834	Magherafelt – 1st 1703 Union Road 1868 Castledawson 1809	M. Magherafelt 1825
41	Tamlaght	47	1801	Arboe 1827	Coagh 1839 Ballygoney 1834	
42	Tamlaght Finlagan	9	1796	Limavady 1855	Ballykelly 1669 Myroe 1850	
43	Tamlaght O'Crilly	35		Greenlough 1846	Boveedy 1841	
44	Tamlaghtard	7	1747	Magilligan 1863	Magilligan 1814	
45	Templemore	24	St. Columbs Cathedral 1642 Christ Church 1855 Culmore 1867	Long Tower 1823 St. Eugenes Cathedral 1873	Derry – 1st 1815 2nd or Strand 1847 3rd or Great James Street 1837 4th or Carlisle Road 1838 Ballyarnet	R.P. Londonderry M. Londonderry, Carlisle Road 1820 C. Londonderry
46	Termoneeny	38	1821	Maghera 1841 Termoneeny 1837		

NGA No.	CIVIL PARISH	GV No.	CHURCH OF IRELAND	ROMAN CATHOLIC	PRESBYTERIAN	OTHERS
1	Abbeylara	7		Abbeylara 1854		
2	Abbeyshrule	23	& Tashinney 1821	Taghshiney, Taghshinod & Abbeyshrule (Carrickedmond) 1835		
3	Agharra	24		Kilglass (Legan) 1855		
4	Ardagh	9	1811	Ardagh & Moydow 1793		
5	Ballymacormick	14		Templemichael & Ballymacormick 1802		
6	Cashel	19		Cashel 1850		
7	Clonbroney	5	1821	Clonbroney 1849		
8	Clongesh	3	1820	Clonguish 1829		
9	Columbkille	4		Columcille 1845 Scrabby & Columcille East 1833		
10	Forgney	25	1803	Moyvore 1831		
11	Granard	6	1820	Granard 1779	Tully 1844 (united with Corboy)	
12	Kilcommock	20	1795	Kilcommuck 1859		
13	Kilglass	16		Kilglass (Legan) 1855		
14	Killashee	13	1771	Killashee 1826		
15	Killoe	1		Killoe 1826 Dromard 1835 Drumlish 1834	Corboy 1839	
16	Mohill	2		Mohill-Manachain 1836		
17	Mostrim	10	1801	Mostrim 1838		
18	Moydow	15	1794	Ardagh & Moydow 1793		
19	Noughaval	26		Drumraney 1834		
20	Rathcline	18		Rathcline 1850		
21	Rathreagh	12		Kilglass (Legan) 1855		
22	Shrule	21		Shrule 1820		
23	Street	11	1801	Streete 1820		

COUNTY LONGFORD

NGA No.	CIVIL PARISH	GV No.	CHURCH OF IRELAND	ROMAN CATHOLIC	PRESBYTERIAN	OTHERS
24	Taghsheenod	17		Taghshiney, Taghshinod & Abbeyshrule (Carrickedmond) 1835		
25	Taghshinny	22	& Abbeyshrule 1821	Taghshiney, Taghshinod & Abbeyshrule 1835		
26	Templemichael	8	1795	Templemichael & Ballymacormick 1802	Longford 1834	M. Longford

NGA No.	CIVIL PARISH	GV No.	CHURCH OF IRELAND	ROMAN CATHOLIC	PRESBYTERIAN	OTHERS
1	Ardee	29	1735	Ardee 1763		
2	Ballybarrack	14		Kilkerley & Haggardstown 1752		
3	Ballyboys	3		Lordship & Ballymascanlan 1838		
4	Ballymakenny	62		Monasterboice 1814 Termonfeckin 1823		
5	Ballymascanlan	1	1808	Lordship & Ballymascanlan 1838 Faughart 1851		
6	Barronstown	10		Kilkerley & Haggardstown 1752		
7	Beaulieu	61		Termonfeckin 1823		
8	Cappoge	38		Dunleer 1772		
9	Carlingford	2		Carlingford 1835 Cooley (South Carlingford) 1811		
10	Carrickbaggot	51		Clogherhead 1742		
11	Castletown	11		Dundalk 1790		
12	Charlestown	27	1822	Tallanstown 1816		
13	Clogher	57		Clogherhead 1742		
14	Clonkeehan	21		Tallanstown 1816		
15	Clonkeen	26	1808	Tallanstown 1816		
16	Clonmore	46		Togher 1791		
17	Collon	48	1790	Collon 1789		
18	Creggan	6		Creggan Upper 1796		
19	Darver	20		Darver 1787		
20	Dromin	37		Dunleer 1772		
21	Dromiskin	19	1802	Darver 1787		
22	Drumcar	35		Togher 1791		
23	Drumshallon	55		Monasterboice 1814 Termonfeckin 1823		

COUNTY LOUTH

NGA No.	CIVIL PARISH	GV No.	CHURCH OF IRELAND	ROMAN CATHOLIC	PRESBYTERIAN	OTHERS
24	Dunany	43		Togher 1791		
25	Dunbin	13		Kilkerley & Haggardstown 1752		
26	Dundalk	12	1729	Dundalk 1790	Dundalk 1819	
27	Dunleer	44		Dunleer 1772		
28	Dysart	45		Togher 1791		
29	Faughart	5		Faughart 1851		
30	Gernonstown	32		Kilsaran 1809	Castlebell-ingham (united with Dundalk 1926)	
31	Haggardstown	15		Kilkerley & Haggardstown 1752		
32	Haynestown	16		Kilkerley & Haggardstown 1752		
33	Inishkeen	9		Inniskeen 1837		
34	Jonesborough	29 Arm-agh	1812	Faughart 1851	Jonesborough 1861	
35	Kane	8		Dundalk 1790		
36	Kildemock	40		Ardee 1763		
37	Killanny	23	1825	Louth 1833 Carrickmacross 1838		
38	Killincoole	18		Darver 1787		
39	Kilsaran	31	1818	Kilsaran 1809		
40	Louth	17		Louth 1833		
41	Mansfieldstown	22	1825	Darver 1787		
42	Mapastown	28		Ardee 1763		
43	Marlestown	50		Clogherhead 1742		
44	Mayne	56		Clogherhead 1742		
45	Monasterboice	54		Monasterboice 1814		
46	Mosstown	41		Dunleer 1772		
47	Mullary	49		Monasterboice 1814		
48	Parsonstown	53		Clogherhead 1742		

NGA No.	CIVIL PARISH	GV No.	CHURCH OF IRELAND	ROMAN CATHOLIC	PRESBYTERIAN	OTHERS
49	Philipstown	7, 24, 59		Kilkerley & Haggardstown 1752 Tallanstown 1816 St. Peter's, Drogheda 1744		
50	Port	47		Togher 1791		
51	Rathdrumin	52		Clogherhead 1742		
52	Richardstown	34		Dunleer 1772		
53	Roche	4		Dundalk 1790		
54	St. Mary's	64	St. Mary's, Drogheda 1811	St. Mary's, Drogheda 1835	Drogheda 1822	M. Drogheda Q. Drogheda
55	St. Peter's	63	St. Peter's, Drogheda 1654	St. Peter's, Drogheda 1744		
56	Salterstown	42		Togher 1791		
57	Shanlis	36		Ardee 1763		
58	Smarmore	39		Ardee 1763		
59	Stabannan	30	1688	Kilsaran 1809		
60	Stickillin	33		Ardee 1763		
61	Tallanstown	25		Tallanstown 1816		
62	Termonfeckin	60		Termonfeckin 1823		
63	Tullyallen	58	& Mellifont 1812	Mellifont 1821		

NGA No.	CIVIL PARISH	GV No.	CHURCH OF IRELAND	ROMAN CATHOLIC	PRESBYTERIAN	OTHERS
1	Achill	19	1854 Dugort 1838	Achill 1867		
2	Addergoole	16		Addergoole 1840		
3	Aghagower	48	1825 Knappagh 1855	Aghagower 1828		
4	Aghamore	70		Aghamore 1864		
5	Aglish	24	Castlebar 1759	Aglish, Ballyheane & Breaghwy (Castlebar) 1824	Castlebar 1846	M. Castlebar
6	Annagh	73		Annagh 1851		
7	Ardagh	14		Ardagh 1870		
8	Attymass	36		Attymass 1874		
9	Balla	59		Balla & Manulla 1837		
10	Ballinachalla	52	or The Neale 1831	Cong & Neale 1870		
11	Ballinrobe	50	1796	Ballinrobe 1843		
12	Ballintober	30		Burriscarra & Ballintubber 1839		
13	Ballyhean	27		Aglish, Ballyheane & Breaghwy (Castlebar) 1824		
14	Ballynahaglish	18		Backs (Rathduff) 1848 Backs (Knockmore) 1854		
15	Ballyovey	34		Ballyovey 1869		
16	Ballysakeery	12	1802	Ballysokeary 1843		
17	Bekan	72		Bekan 1832		
18	Bohola	43		Bohola 1857		
19	Breaghwy	26		Aglish, Ballyheane & Breaghwy (Castlebar) 1824		
20	Burriscarra	31		Burriscarra & Ballintubber 1839		

NGA No.	CIVIL PARISH	GV No.	CHURCH OF IRELAND	ROMAN CATHOLIC	PRESBYTERIAN	OTHERS
21	Burrishoole	20		Burrishoole 1872	Newport 1857 (united with Westport 1890)	Q. Newport
22	Cong	55	1811	Cong & Neale 1870		
23	Crossboyne	63		Crossboyne & Tagheen 1862		
24	Crossmolina	13	1768	Crossmolina 1831		
25	Doonfeeny	3		Ballycastle 1864	Ballinglen 1849 (united with Killala 1915)	
26	Drum	29		Balla & Manulla 1837		
27	Islandeady	23		Islandeady 1839		
28	Kilbeagh	66		Kilbeagh (Charlestown) 1845 Carracastle 1847		
29	Kilbelfad	17		Backs (Rathduff) 1848 Backs (Knock-more) 1854		
30	Kilbride	4		Ballycastle 1864		
31	Kilcolman	61, 67		Kilcolman (Claremorris) 1806 Castlemore & Kilcolman 1830		
32	Kilcommon	2, 51		Ballycroy (No registers before 1880) Belmullet 1836 Kilcommon-Erris (No registers before 1880) Kiltane 1860 Kilcommon & Robeen 1857	Hollymount 1851	
33	Kilconduff	41		Kilconduff & Meelick 1808		
34	Kilcummin	5		Lackan 1852		
35	Kildacommoge	42		Keelogues 1847		
36	Kilfian	7		Kilfian 1826		
37	Kilgarvan	35		Kilgarvan 1844		

NGA No.	CIVIL PARISH	GV No.	CHURCH OF IRELAND	ROMAN CATHOLIC	PRESBYTERIAN	OTHERS
38	Kilgeever	47		Clare Island 1851 Kilgeever 1850		
39	Killala	10	1757	Killala 1852	Killala or Mullaferry 1849	
40	Killasser	38		Killasser 1847		
41	Killedan	44		Killedan 1834		
42	Kilmaclasser	22		Kilmeena 1858		
43	Kilmainebeg	56		Kilmaine 1854		
44	Kilmainemore	54	1744	Kilmaine 1854		
45	Kilmeena	21		Kilmeena 1858		
46	Kilmolara	53		Cong & Neale 1870		
47	Kilmore	1		Belmullet 1836 Kilmore-Erris 1860		
48	Kilmoremoy	15	1801	Kilmoremoy 1823	Ballina 1846 (By 1919 new grouping of Ballina, West-port, Newport, Castlebar & Hollymount)	M. Ballina B. Ballina
49	Kilmovee	68		Kilmovee 1824		
50	Kilturra	65		Kilshalvey 1840		
51	Kilvine	64		Kilvine (No registers be-fore 1880)		
52	Knock	71		Knock 1868		
53	Lackan	6		Lackan 1852		
54	Manulla	28		Balla & Manulla 1837		
55	Mayo	60		Mayo Abbey 1841		
56	Meelick	40		Kilconduff & Meelick 1808		
57	Moorgagagh	57		Kilmaine 1854		
58	Moygawnagh	11	1802	Moygownagh (No registers be-fore 1880)		
59	Oughaval	45	or Westport 1801	Aughaval 1823	Westport 1846	
60	Rathreagh	8		Kilfian 1826		

NGA No.	CIVIL PARISH	GV No.	CHURCH OF IRELAND	ROMAN CATHOLIC	PRESBYTERIAN	OTHERS
61	Robeen	49		Kilcommon & Robeen 1857		
62	Rosslee	32		Mayo Abbey 1841		
63	Shrule	58		Shrule 1831		
64	Tagheen	62		Crossboyne & Tagheen 1862		
65	Templemore	39	or Straid 1755	Templemore (Straide) 1872		
66	Templemurry	9		Killala 1852		
67	Toomore	37		Toomore (Foxford) 1833		
68	Touaghty	33		Burriscarra & Ballintubber 1839		
69	Turlough	25	1821	Turlough 1847	Turlough (united with Castlebar 1863)	

NGA No.	CIVIL PARISH	GV No.	CHURCH OF IRELAND	ROMAN CATHOLIC	PRESBYTERIAN	OTHERS
1	Agher	138		Summerhill 1812		
2	Ardagh	17		Drumconrath 1811		
3	Ardbraccan	50		Bohermeen 1831		
4	Ardcath	102		Ardcath 1795		
5	Ardmulchan	79		Blacklion (Yellow Furze) 1815		
6	Ardsallagh	57		Navan 1782		
7	Assey	116		Kilmessan & Dunsany 1742		
8	Athboy	70	1736	Athboy 1794		
9	Athlumney	80		Johnstown 1839		
10	Balfeaghan	141		Batterstown (Kilcloon) 1836		
11	Ballyboggan	110		Ballinabrackey 1826		
12	Ballygarth	100		Stamullen 1830		
13	Ballymagarvey	68		Blacklion (Yellow Furze) 1815		
14	Ballymaglassan	135	1800	Batterstown (Kilcloon) 1836		
15	Balrathboyne	36		Bohermeen 1831		
16	Balsoon	117		Kilmessan & Dunsany 1742		
17	Bective	76	1853	Dunderry 1837		
18	Brownstown	84		Blacklion (Yellow Furze) 1815		
19	Burry	35		Kells 1791		
20	Castlejordan	111		Ballinabrackey 1826		
21	Castlekeeran or Loughan	32		Carnaross 1806		
22	Castlerickard	108	1869	Ballivor & Kildalkey 1837 Longwood 1829		
23	Castletown	11		Castletown 1805		
24	Churchtown	55		Dunderry 1837		
25	Clonalvy	106		Ardcath 1795		
26	Clonard	109	1792	Longwood 1829		

NGA No.	CIVIL PARISH	GV No.	CHURCH OF IRELAND	ROMAN CATHOLIC	PRESBYTERIAN	OTHERS
27	Clongill	15		Castletown 1805		
28	Clonmacduff	73		Dunderry 1837		
29	Collon	43	1790	Collon 1789		
30	Colp	61		St. Mary's, Drogheda 1835		
31	Cookstown	129		Ratoath & Ashbourne 1780		
32	Crickstown	128		Curraha 1802		
33	Cruicetown	5		Nobber 1754		
34	Culmullin	137		Dunshaughlin 1789		
35	Cushinstown	99		Duleek 1852		
36	Danestown	88		Blacklion (Yellow Furze) 1815		
37	Derrypatrick	123		Moynalvy & Galtrim 1783		
38	Diamor	29		Kilskyre 1784		
39	Donaghmore	52, 133		Navan 1782 Collon 1789		
40	Donaghpatrick	38		Oristown 1757		
41	Donore	59		Rosnaree & Donore 1840		
42	Dowdstown	85		Skyrne 1841		
43	Dowth	48		Slane 1851		
44	Drakestown	12		Castletown 1805		
45	Drumcondra	18	Drumconrath 1799	Drumconrath 1811		
46	Drumlargan	139		Summerhill 1812		
47	Dulane	33		Carnaross 1806		
48	Duleek	64		Duleek 1852		
49	Duleek Abbey	103		Duleek 1852		
50	Dunboyne	145		Dunboyne 1787		
51	Dunmoe	53		Slane 1851		
52	Dunsany	95		Kilmessan & Dunsany 1742		
53	Dunshaughlin	126	1800	Dunshaughlin 1789		
54	Emlagh	7		Carolanstown (Kilbeg) 1810		

NGA No.	CIVIL PARISH	GV No.	CHURCH OF IRELAND	ROMAN CATHOLIC	PRESBYTERIAN	OTHERS
55	Enniskeen	9		Enniskeen 1838	Ervey	
56	Fennor	58		Slane 1851		
57	Follistown	82		Johnstown 1839		
58	Gallow	140		Summerhill 1812		
59	Galtrim	121		Moynalvy & Galtrim 1783		
60	Gernonstown	41		Rathkenny 1784		
61	Girley	39		Kells 1791		
62	Grangegeeth	42		Rathkenny 1784		
63	Greenoge	134		Curraha 1802		
64	Inishmot	20		Lobinstown 1823		
65	Julianstown	66		Stamullen 1830		
66	Kells	34	1773	Kells 1791	Kells	
67	Kentstown	67		Blacklion (Yellow Furze) 1815		
68	Kilbeg	4		Carolanstown (Kilbeg) 1810		
69	Kilberry	16		Oristown 1757		
70	Kilbrew	125		Curraha 1802		
71	Kilbride	24, 146		Kilbride 1787 Dunboyne 1787		
72	Kilcarn	81		Johnstown 1839		
73	Kilclone	143		Batterstown (Kilcloon) 1836		
74	Kilcooly	78		Dunderry 1837		
75	Kildalkey	71		Ballivor & Kildalkey 1837		
76	Killaconnigan	72	Killochanagan 1853	Ballivor & Kildalkey 1837		
77	Killallon	30		Clonmellon 1757		
78	Killary	23		Lobinstown 1823		
79	Killeagh	26		Kilbride 1787		
80	Killeen	94		Kilmessan & Dunsany 1742		
81	Killegland	130		Ratoath & Ashbourne 1780		
82	Killyon	107		Ballivor & Kildalkey 1837 Longwood 1829		

COUNTY MEATH

NGA No.	CIVIL PARISH	GV No.	CHURCH OF IRELAND	ROMAN CATHOLIC	PRESBYTERIAN	OTHERS
83	Kilmainham	2		Kilmainham & Moybologue 1867		C. Kilmainham
84	Kilmessan	120		Kilmessan & Dunsany 1742		
85	Kilmoon	98		Curraha 1802		
86	Kilmore	136	1859	Moynalvy & Galtrim 1783		
87	Kilsharvan	65		St. Mary's, Drogheda 1835		
88	Kilshine	14		Castletown 1805		
89	Kilskeer	31		Kilskyre 1784		
90	Kiltale	122		Moynalvy & Galtrim 1783		
91	Knock	13		Castletown 1805		
92	Knockcommon	63		Rosnaree & Donore 1840		
93	Knockmark	124	1825	Dunshaughlin 1789		
94	Laracor	113		Summerhill 1812	Summerhill	
95	Liscartan	51		Bohermeen 1831		
96	Lismullin	90		Skyrne 1841		
97	Loughbrackan	19		Drumconrath 1811		
98	Loughcrew	28		Oldcastle 1789		
99	Macetown	97		Skyrne 1841		
100	Martry	49		Bohermeen 1831		
101	Mitchelstown	21		Lobinstown 1823		
102	Monknewtown	47		Slane 1851		
103	Monktown	87		Johnstown 1839		
104	Moorechurch	101		Stamullen 1830		
105	Moybolgue	1		Kilmainham & Moybologue 1867		
106	Moyglare	144		Batterstown (Kilcloon) 1836		
107	Moylagh	27		Oldcastle 1789		
108	Moymet	75		Dunderry 1837		
109	Moynalty	3		Moynalty 1829		
110	Navan	54	1870	Navan 1782		
111	Newtown	6		Moynalty 1829		

NGA No.	CIVIL PARISH	GV No.	CHURCH OF IRELAND	ROMAN CATHOLIC	PRESBYTERIAN	OTHERS
112	Newtownclonbun	77		Trim 1829		
113	Nobber	10	1828	Nobber 1754		
114	Oldcastle	25	1814	Oldcastle 1789		
115	Painestown	62	1698	Blacklion (Yellow Furze) 1815		
116	Piercetown	105		Ardcath 1795 Duleek 1852		
117	Rataine	56		Dunderry 1837		
118	Rathbeggan	132	1821	Ratoath & Ashbourne 1780		
119	Rathcore	115	1810	Rathcore & Rathmolyon Longwood 1829		
120	Rathfeigh	92		Skyrne 1841		
121	Rathkenny	40		Rathkenny 1784		
122	Rathmolyon	114		Rathcore & Rathmolyon		
123	Rathmore	69		Athboy 1794		
124	Rathregan	131		Batterstown (Kilcloon) 1836		
125	Ratoath	127		Ratoath & Ashbourne 1780		
126	Rodanstown	142		Batterstown (Kilcloon) 1836		
127	St. Mary's	60	Drogheda 1811	St. Mary's, Drogheda 1835	Drogheda	M. Drogheda Q. Drogheda
128	Scurlockstown	119		Kilmessan & Dunsany 1742		
129	Siddan	22	1720	Lobinstown 1823		
130	Skreen	91		Skyrne 1841		
131	Slane	44		Slane 1851		
132	Stackallan	46		Rathkenny 1754 Slane 1851		
133	Staffordstown	83		Johnstown 1839		
134	Staholmog	8		Carolanstown (Kilbeg) 1810		
135	Stamullin	104		Stamullen 1830		
136	Tara	89		Skyrne 1841		
137	Teltown	37		Oristown 1757		
138	Templekeeran	86		Skyrne 1841		

COUNTY MEATH

NGA No.	CIVIL PARISH	GV No.	CHURCH OF IRELAND	ROMAN CATHOLIC	PRESBYTERIAN	OTHERS
139	Timoole	93		Blacklion (Yellow Furze) 1815		
140	Trevet	96		Skyrne 1841		
141	Trim	112	1836	Trim 1829		
142	Trubley	118		Kilmessan & Dunsany 1742		
143	Tullaghanoge	74		Dunderrry 1837		
144	Tullyallen	45	& Mellifont 1812	Collon 1789		

NGA No.	CIVIL PARISH	GV No.	CHURCH OF IRELAND	ROMAN CATHOLIC	PRESBYTERIAN	OTHERS
1	Aghabog	12		Aghabog 1856	Drumkeen 1856	
2	Aghnamullen	18		Aughnamullen West 1841 Aughnamullen East 1857	Creeve 1819 Loughmourne 1846 Corlea 1835	
3	Ballybay	17	1813	Tullycorbet 1862	Ballybay – 1st 1834 2nd 1833 Derryvalley 1816	R.P. Crevagh & Fairview
4	Clones	9	1682 Aghadrumsee 1821 Clough 1811	Clones 1821	Clones 1856 Ballyhobridge 1846 Smithborough 1868 Stonebridge 1821	M. Clones
5	Clontibret	15	1864	Clontibret 1861	Clontibret – 1st 1825 2nd or Braddox 1856 (united 1903)	
6	Currin	13	1810 Currin Drum 1828	Drummully 1845	Drum – 1st 1866 2nd 1868 (united 1881)	
7	Donagh	2	1796	Donagh 1836	Glennan or Glaslough 1805 Emyvale or Carrigans.	
8	Donaghmoyne	20		Donaghmoyne 1863	Broomfield 1841	
9	Drummully	11	1802	Drummully 1845		
10	Drumsnat	5	1825	Drumsnat & Kilmore 1836		
11	Ematris	14	1753	Ematris 1848	Rockcorry	S.P. Rockcorry
12	Errigal Trough	1	1809	Errigal Trough 1835		
13	Inishkeen	21		Donaghmoyne 1863		
14	Killanny	23	1825	Killany 1857		
15	Killeevan	10	1811 Newbliss 1841	Killevan 1871	Newbliss 1856	
16	Kilmore	6	1796	Drumsnat & Kilmore 1836		
17	Magheracloone	22	1806	Magheracloone 1826		
18	Magheross	19	or Carrickmacross 1796 Ardragh (St. Patricks) 1865	Maghaire Rois 1838	Carrickmaclim or Corvally 1832	

NGA No.	CIVIL PARISH	GV No.	CHURCH OF IRELAND	ROMAN CATHOLIC	PRESBYTERIAN	OTHERS
19	Monaghan	7	1802	Monaghan 1827	Monaghan – 1st 1821 2nd or Bally-albany 1802	M. Monaghan B. Monaghan Q. Castleshane
20	Muckno	16	(Castleblayney) 1810	Muckno 1835	Castleblayney – 1st 1832 2nd or Frank-ford 1820 (united 1929)	S.P. Garmoney Grove
21	Tedavnet	3	Tydavnet 1822 Mullaghfad 1836	Tydavnet 1825	Scotstown 1855	
22	Tehallan	4	or Tyholland 1806	Tyholland 1827		
23	Tullycorbet	8	1796	Tullycorbet 1862	Cahans 1752	

NGA No.	CIVIL PARISH	GV No.	CHURCH OF IRELAND	ROMAN CATHOLIC	PRESBYTERIAN	OTHERS
1	Aghancon	38		Seirkieran 1830		
2	Ardnurcher or Horseleap	3		Clara 1821		
3	Ballyboy	27	or Frankford 1796	Kilcormac 1821		
4	Ballyburly	6		Rhode 1829		
5	Ballycommon	21		Daingean 1795		
6	Ballykean	29		Killeigh 1844		
7	Ballymacwilliam	7		Rhode 1829		
8	Ballynakill	24		Edenderry 1820 Clonbulloge 1808		
9	Birr	34	1772	Birr 1838	Birr (united with Tullamore 1938)	B. Parsonstown Q. Birr
10	Borrisnafarney	51	1827	Couraganeen 1836		
11	Castlejordan	5	1823	Ballinabrackey 1826 Rhode 1829		
12	Castletownely	48		Dunkerrin 1820		
13	Clonmacnoise	8	1828	Clonmacnoise 1826 Lemanaghan & Ballynahowen 1821		
14	Clonsast	25	1805	Clonbulloge 1808		
15	Clonyhurk	30	1824	Portarlington 1820		
16	Corbally	40	1834	Couraganeen 1836		
17	Croghan	19		Rhode 1829		
18	Cullenwaine	50		Dunkerrin 1820		
19	Drumcullen	32		Eglish 1809		
20	Dunkerrin	46	1800	Dunkerrin 1820		
21	Durrow	15	1816	Tullamore 1801		
22	Eglish	31		Eglish 1809		
23	Ettagh	43	1825	Kilcolman 1830		
24	Finglass	49		Dunkerrin 1820		
25	Gallen	12	1842	Gallen & Reynagh 1797		

NGA No.	CIVIL PARISH	GV No.	CHURCH OF IRELAND	ROMAN CATHOLIC	PRESBYTERIAN	OTHERS
26	Geashill	28	1713 Killeigh 1835	Clonbulloge 1808 Killeigh 1844 Portarlington 1820		
27	Kilbride	4, 17	(Tullamore) 1805	Clara 1821 Tullamore 1801	Tullamore	M. Tullamore
28	Kilclonfert	20	Daingean 1795			
29	Kilcolman	41	1839	Kilcolman 1830		
30	Kilcomin	45		Shinrone 1842		
31	Kilcumreragh	1		Kilcleagh & Ballyloughloe (Moate & Colry) 1823		
32	Killaderry	22		Daingean 1795		
33	Killagally or Wheery	11	Ferbane 1819	Tisaran & Fuithre 1819		B. Ferbane
34	Killoughy	26		Kilcormac 1821		
35	Kilmanaghan	2		Kilcleagh & Ballyloughloe (Moate & Colry) 1823		
36	Kilmurryely	42		Shinrone 1842		
37	Kinnitty	36	1800	Kinnitty 1833		
38	Lemanaghan	9		Lemanaghan & Ballynahowen 1821		
39	Letterluna	33		Kinnitty 1833		
40	Lusmagh	14		Lusmagh 1824		
41	Lynally	18		Killina (Rahan) 1810		
42	Monasteroris	23	1698	Edenderry 1820		Q. Edenderry
43	Rahan	16		Killina (Rahan) 1810		
44	Reynagh	13		Gallen & Reynagh 1797		
45	Roscomroe	37		Kinnitty 1833		
46	Roscrea	39	1784	Roscrea & Corbally 1810		
47	Seirkieran	35		Seirkieran 1830		
48	Shinrone	44	1741	Shinrone 1842		
49	Templeharry	47	1800	Dunkerrin 1820		
50	Tisaran	10	1819	Tisaran & Fuithre 1819		

COUNTY ROSCOMMON

NGA No.	CIVIL PARISH	GV No.	CHURCH OF IRELAND	ROMAN CATHOLIC	PRESBYTERIAN	OTHERS
1	Ardcarn	4	1820	Ardcarne 1843		
2	Athleague	44		Athleague & Fuerty 1808		
3	Aughrim	19		Aughrim 1816		
4	Ballintober	18		Ballintober & Ballymoe 1831		
5	Ballynakill	35		Glinsk & Kilbegnet 1836		
6	Baslick	16		Ogulla & Baslick 1864		
7	Boyle	2	1793	Boyle & Kilbryan 1792	Boyle	M. Boyle B. Boyle
8	Bumlin	26	1811	Kiltrustan, Lissonuffy & Cloonfinlough 1830		
9	Cam	51		Kiltoom 1835		
10	Castlemore	9B		Castlemore & Kilcolman 1830		
11	Clooncraff	21		Aughrim 1816 Kilmore 1825		
12	Cloonfinlough	28		Kiltrustan, Lissonuffy & Cloonfinlough 1830		
13	Cloontuskert	40		Cloontuskert, Kilgeffin & Curraghroe 1865		
14	Cloonygormican	34		Glinsk & Kilbegnet 1836		
15	Creagh	57	1823	Creagh 1820		
16	Creeve	13		Elphin & Creeve 1807		
17	Drum	56		Athlone, St. Peter's & Drum 1789		
18	Drumatemple	33		Oran (Cloverhill) 1845		
19	Dunamon	37		Glinsk & Kilbegnet 1836		
20	Dysart	53		Dysert & Tissara 1850		
21	Elphin	22		Elphin & Creeve 1807		Q. Ballymurry

COUNTY ROSCOMMON

NGA No.	CIVIL PARISH	GV No.	CHURCH OF IRELAND	ROMAN CATHOLIC	PRESBYTERIAN	OTHERS
22	Esternow	6	1800	Kilnamanagh & Esternow 1859		
23	Fuerty	43		Athleague & Fuerty 1808		
24	Kilbride	38		Cloontuskert, Kilgeffin & Curraghroe 1865 Kilbride 1835		
25	Kilbryan	3	1852	Boyle & Kilbryan 1792		
26	Kilcolagh	11	.	Killucan 1811 Kilnamanagh & Esternow 1859		
27	Kilcolman	9A		Castlemore & Kilcolman 1830		
28	Kilcooley	25		Killucan 1811		
29	Kilcorkey	14		Kilcorkey & Frenchpark 1865		
30	Kilgefin	39		Cloontuskert, Kilgeffin & Curraghroe 1865		
31	Kilglass	31	1823	Kilglass & Rooskey 1865		
32	Kilkeevin	15	1748	Kilkeevan 1804		
33	Killinvoy	46		St. John's 1841		
34	Killukin	7, 27	Croghan 1862	Killucan 1811		
35	Killummod	8		Killucan 1811		
36	Kilmacumsy	12		Elphin & Creeve 1807		
37	Kilmeane	45		St. John's 1841		
38	Kilmore	30		Kilmore 1825		
39	Kilnamanagh	9		Kilnamanagh & Esternow 1859		
40	Kilronan	1		Kilronan 1823		
41	Kilteevan	42		Roscommon & Kilteevan 1820		
42	Kiltoom	52	1797	Kiltoom 1835		
43	Kiltrustan	23		Kiltrustan, Lissonuffy & Cloonfinlough 1830		
44	Kiltullagh	17	1822	Kiltullagh 1839		

COUNTY ROSCOMMON

NGA No.	CIVIL PARISH	GV No.	CHURCH OF IRELAND	ROMAN CATHOLIC	PRESBYTERIAN	OTHERS
45	Lissonuffy	29		Kiltrustan, Lissonuffy & Cloonfinlough 1830		
46	Moore	58		Moore 1876 Creagh 1820		
47	Ogulla	24		Ogulla & Baslick 1864		
48	Oran	36		Oran (Cloverhill) 1845		
49	Rahara	48		St. John's 1841		
50	Roscommon	41		Roscommon & Kilteevan 1820	Roscommon 1867 (united with Creggs 1873 and with Athlone 1925)	
51	St. John's	49		St. John's 1841		
52	St. Peter's	55		Athlone, St. Peter's & Drum 1789	Athlone	M. Athlone Q. Athlone
53	Shankill	20		Elphin & Creeve 1807		
54	Taghboy	50		Dysert & Tissara 1850		
55	Taghmaconnell	54	(with Creagh) 1855	Taghmaconnell 1842		
56	Termonbarry	32		Kilglass & Rooskey 1865		
57	Tibohine	10		Tibohine 1833 Loughglynn 1817		
58	Tisrara	47		Dysert & Tissara 1850		
59	Tumna	5		Ardcarne 1843 Killucan 1811		

COUNTY SLIGO

NGA No.	CIVIL PARISH	GV No.	CHURCH OF IRELAND	ROMAN CATHOLIC	PRESBYTERIAN	OTHERS
1	Achonry	19		Cloonacool 1859 Achonry 1865 Curry 1867		
2	Aghanagh	38	1856	Aghanagh 1800		
3	Ahamlish	1	1811	Ahamlish 1796		
4	Ballynakill	31		Riverstown 1803		
5	Ballysadare	16		Ballisodare & Kilvarnet 1842		
6	Ballysumaghan	30	1828	Riverstown 1803		
7	Calry	4		Sligo, Coolera, Calry, Rosses Point & St. Mary's 1858		
8	Castleconor	14	1800	Castleconor 1854		
9	Cloonoghil	23		Kilshalvey, Kilturra & Cloonoghill 1840		
10	Dromard	13		Skreen & Dromard 1817		
11	Drumcliff	3	1805 Lissadill 1836	Drumcliffe 1841		
12	Drumcolumb	32		Riverstown 1803		
13	Drumrat	27		Drumrat 1842		
14	Easky	9	1822	Easky 1864		B. Easky
15	Emlaghfad	21	1831	Emlefad & Kilmorgan 1824	Ballymote (united with Boyle 1929)	
16	Kilcolman	40		Castlemore & Kilcolman 1830		
17	Kilfree	39		Kilfree & Killaraght 1844		
18	Kilglass	8		Kilglass 1825		
19	Killadoon	35		Geevagh 1851		
20	Killaraght	41		Kilfree & Killaraght 1844		
21	Killaspugbrone	5	Knocknarea 1842	Sligo, Coolera, Calry, Rosses Point & St. Mary's 1858		
22	Killerry	28		Killenummery & Killerry 1827		
23	Killoran	17		Killoran 1846		
24	Kilmacallan	34		Riverstown 1803		

NGA No.	CIVIL PARISH	GV No.	CHURCH OF IRELAND	ROMAN CATHOLIC	PRESBYTERIAN	OTHERS
25	Kilmacowen	7		Sligo, Coolera, Calry, Rosses Point & St. Mary's 1858		
26	Kilmacshalgan	10		Kilmacshalgan 1815	Dromore West 1849	
27	Kilmacteige	20		Kilmacteigue 1845		
28	Kilmactranny	37	1816	Geevagh 1851		
29	Kilmoremoy	15		Kilmoremoy 1823		
30	Kilmorgan	22		Emlefad & Kilmorgan 1824		
31	Kilross	29		Riverstown 1803		
32	Kilshalvy	26		Kilshalvey, Kilturra & Cloonoghill 1840		
33	Kilturra	25		Kilshalvey, Kilturra & Cloonoghill 1840		
34	Kilvarnet	18		Ballisodare & Kilvarnet 1842		
35	Rossinver	2		Rossinver 1844 Glenade 1867 Kinlough 1835		
36	St. John's	6	St. John, Sligo 1802	Sligo, Coolera, Calry, Rosses Point & St. Mary's 1858	Sligo 1824	M. Sligo C. Sligo
37	Shancough	36		Geevagh 1851		
38	Skreen	12		Skreen & Dromard 1817		
39	Tawnagh	33		Riverstown 1803		
40	Templeboy	11		Templeboy 1815		
41	Toomour	24		Tumore 1833		

NGA No.	CIVIL PARISH	GV No.	CHURCH OF IRELAND	ROMAN CATHOLIC	PRESBYTERIAN	OTHERS
1	Abington	28 N		Murroe & Boher 1814		
2	Aghnameadle	38 N	1834	Toomevara 1830		
3	Aglishcloghane	4 N		Borrisokane 1821		
4	Ardcrony	13 N		Cloughjordan 1833		
5	Athnid	71 N		Thurles 1795		
6	Ballingarry	10 N	1816	Borrisokane 1821		
7	Ballycahill	68 N		Holycross 1835		
8	Ballygibbon	29 N		Toomevara 1830		
9	Ballymackey	31 N		Toomevara 1830		
10	Ballymurreen	79 N		Moycarky 1793		
11	Ballynaclogh	36 N		Silvermines 1840		
12	Barnane-ely	51 N		Drom & Inch 1827		
13	Borrisnafarney	47 N	1827	Couraganeen 1836		
14	Borrisokane	8 N		Borrisokane 1821		
15	Bourney	45 N		Couraganeen 1836		
16	Burgesbeg	22 N		Burgess & Youghal 1820		
17	Castletownarra	19 N	1802	Castletownarra (Portroe) 1849		
18	Cloghprior	12 N		Cloghprior & Monsea 1834		
19	Corbally	43 N	1834	Couraganeen 1836		
20	Cullenwaine	46 N		Dunkerrin 1820		
21	Dolla	35 N		Silvermines 1840 Killanave & Templederry 1839		

NGA No.	CIVIL PARISH	GV No.	CHURCH OF IRELAND	ROMAN CATHOLIC	PRESBYTERIAN	OTHERS
22	Doon	57 N		Doon 1824		
23	Dorrha	2 N		Lorrha		
24	Drom	62 N		Drom & Inch 1827		
25	Dromineer	15 N		Cloghprior & Monsea 1834		
26	Fertiana	74 N		Moycarky 1793		
27	Finnoe	7 N		Kilbarron & Terryglass 1827		
28	Galbooly	75 N		Moycarky 1793		
29	Glenkeen	54 N		Drom & Inch 1827 Killanave & Templederry 1839 Borrisoleigh 1814		
30	Holycross	73 N, 35 S	1784	Holycross 1835		
31	Inch	66 N		Drom & Inch 1827		
32	Kilbarron	6 N		Kilbarron & Terryglass 1827		
33	Kilclonagh	67 N		Templetuohy 1804		
34	Kilcomenty	24 N		Newwport 1795		
35	Kilcooly	77 N		Gortnahoe 1805		
36	Kilfithmone	61 N	1792	Drom & Inch 1827		
37	Kilkeary	37 N		Toomevara 1830		
38	Killavinoge	49 N		Templemore 1807		
39	Killea	48 N		Templemore 1807		
40	Killodiernan	11 N		Cloghprior & Monsea 1834		

NGA No.	CIVIL PARISH	GV No.	CHURCH OF IRELAND	ROMAN CATHOLIC	PRESBYTERIAN	OTHERS
41	Killoscully	25 N		Newport 1795 Ballinahinch 1839		
42	Killoskehan	50 N		Drom & Inch 1827		
43	Kilmastulla	23 N	& Templecalla 1799	Ballina 1832		
44	Kilmore	34 N		Silvermines 1840		
45	Kilnaneave	39 N		Killanave & Templederry 1839		
46	Kilnarath	27 N		Newport 1795		
47	Kilruane	30 N		Cloughjordan 1833		
48	Kilvellane	26 N	St. John, Newport 1782	Newport 1795		
49	Knigh	16 N		Cloghprior & Monsea 1834		
50	Latteragh	40 N		Toomevara 1830		
51	Lisbunny	32 N		Nenagh 1792		
52	Lorrha	1 N		Lorrha		
53	Loughkeen	5 N		Birr 1838		
54	Loughmoe East	64 N		Loughmoe or Loughmore 1798		
55	Loughmoe West	63 N		Loughmoe or Loughmore 1798		
56	Modreeny	14 N	1827 Cloughjordan 1827	Cloughjordan 1833		M. Cloughjordan B. Cloughjordan
57	Monsea	17 N		Cloghprior & Monsea 1834		
58	Moyaliff	59 N	or Mealiffe 1791	Upperchurch 1829		
59	Moycarky	78 N		Moycarky 1793		
60	Moyne	65 N		Templetuohy 1804		
61	Nenagh	18 N		Nenagh 1792		M. Nenagh

NGA No.	CIVIL PARISH	GV No.	CHURCH OF IRELAND	ROMAN CATHOLIC	PRESBYTERIAN	OTHERS
62	Rahelty	72 N		Thurles 1795		
63	Rathnaveoge	64 N		Dunkerrin 1820		
64	Roscrea	42 N		Roscrea & Corbally 1810		M. Roscrea
65	Shyane	70 N		Thurles 1795		
66	Templeachally	21 N	& Kilmastulla 1799	Ballina 1832		
67	Templebeg	56 N		Cappawhite 1804 Upperchurch 1829 Kilcommon 1813		
68	Templederry	41 N		Killanave & Templederry 1839		
69	Templedowney	33 N		Toomevara 1830		
70	Templemore	60 N	1791	Templemore 1807		
71	Templeree	52 N		Loughmoe or Loughmore 1798		
72	Templetouhy	53 N	1789	Templetuohy 1804		
73	Terryglass	3 N	1809	Kilbarron & Terryglass 1827		
74	Thurles	69 N		Thurles 1795		
75	Toem	58 N, 9 S	1802	Cappawhite 1804		
76	Twomileborris	76 N		Moycarky 1793		
77	Upperchurch	55 N		Upperchurch 1829		
78	Uskane	9 N		Borrisokane 1821		
79	Youghalarra	20 N		Burgess & Youghal 1820		

NGA No.	CIVIL PARISH	GV No.	CHURCH OF IRELAND	ROMAN CATHOLIC	PRESBYTERIAN	OTHERS
1	Aghacrew	4 S		Annacarty 1821		
2	Ardfinnan	94 S		Ardfinnan 1809		
3	Ardmayle	37 S	1815	Boherlahan & Dualla 1823		
4	Ballingarry	77 S	1816	Ballingarry 1814		
5	Ballintemple	6 S	1805	Knockavilla 1834		
6	Ballybacon	97 S		Ardfinnan 1809		
7	Ballyclerahan	101 S		Clerihan 1852		
8	Ballygriffin	14 S		Knockavilla 1834		
9	Ballysheehan	38 S		Boherlahan & Dualla 1823		
10	Baptistgrange	68 S		Powerstown 1808		
11	Barrettsgrange	60 S		Fethard & Killusty 1806		
12	Boytonrath	56 S		Golden 1833		
13	Brickendown	43 S		Boherlahan & Dualla 1823		
14	Bruis	27 S		Lattin & Cullen 1846		
15	Buolick	72 S		Gortnahoe 1805		
16	Caher	91 S	1801	Cahir 1776		Q. Kilcommonbeg
17	Carrick	116 S	1803	Carrick-on-Suir 1784		
18	Clogher	1 S		Clonoulty 1804		
19	Clonbeg	33 S		Galbally 1809		
20	Clonbullogue	32 S		Bansha & Kilmoyler 1820		
21	Cloneen	54 S		Drangan 1811		
22	Clonoulty	3 S	1817	Clonoulty 1804 Boherlahan & Dualla 1823		

NGA No.	CIVIL PARISH	GV No.	CHURCH OF IRELAND	ROMAN CATHOLIC	PRESBYTERIAN	OTHERS
23	Clonpet	28 S		Lattin & Cullen 1846		
24	Colman	66 S		Clerihan 1852		
25	Cooleagh	45 S		Killenaule 1742		
26	Coolmundry	63 S		Fethard & Killusty 1806		
27	Cordangan	29 S		Lattin & Cullen 1846		
28	Corroge	25 S		Tipperary 1793		
29	Crohane	78 S		Ballingarry 1814		
30	Cullen	17 S	1770	Lattin & Cullen 1846		
31	Dangandargan	49 S		Golden 1833		
32	Derrygrath	92 S		Ardfinnan 1809		
33	Dogstown	57 S		Golden 1833		
34	Donaghmore	67 S		Powerstown 1808		
35	Donohill	2 S	1856	Annacarty 1821		
36	Drangan	48 S		Drangan 1811		
37	Emly	22 S		Emly 1809		
38	Erry	39 S		Boherlahan & Dualla 1823		
39	Fennor	71 S		Gortnahoe 1805		
40	Fethard	62 S	1804	Fethard & Killusty 1806	Fethard (united with Clonmel 1878)	
41	Gaile	36 S		Boherlahan & Dualla 1823		
42	Garrangibbon	106 S		Ballyneale 1839		
43	Glenbane	23 S		Lattin & Cullen 1846		
44	Grangemockler	84 S		Ballyneale 1839		

NGA No.	CIVIL PARISH	GV No.	CHURCH OF IRELAND	ROMAN CATHOLIC	PRESBYTERIAN	OTHERS
45	Graystown	74 S		Killenaule 1742		
46	Horeabbey	41 S		Cashel 1793		
47	Inishlounaght	102 S	1801	St. Mary's, Clonmel 1790		
48	Isertkieran	82 S		Mullinahone 1809		
49	Kilbragh	59 S		Cashel 1793		
50	Kilcash	107 S		Kilsheelan 1840		
51	Kilconnell	51 S		Boherlahan & Dualla 1823 Killenaule 1742		
52	Kilcooly	73 S		Gortnahoe 1805 Killenaule 1742		B. Kilcooly Hills
53	Kilcornan	16 S		Pallasgreen 1811		
54	Kilfeakle	20 S		Golden 1833		
55	Kilgrant	110 S		Powerstown 1808		
56	Killaloan	115 S		Kilsheelan 1840		
57	Killardry	31 S		Bansha & Kilmoyler 1820		
58	Killeenasteena	55 S		Golden 1833		
59	Killenaule	75 S		Killenaule 1742		
60	Kilmore	7 S		Knockavilla 1834		
61	Kilmucklin	12 S		Tipperary 1793		
62	Kilmurry	112 S		Ballyneale 1839		
63	Kilpatrick	5 S		Knockavilla 1834		
64	Kilshane	30 S		Tipperary 1793		
65	Kilsheelan	111 S		Kilsheelan 1840		

COUNTY TIPPERARY SOUTH

NGA No.	CIVIL PARISH	GV No.	CHURCH OF IRELAND	ROMAN CATHOLIC	PRESBYTERIAN	OTHERS
66	Kiltegan	109 S		Powerstown 1808		
67	Kiltinan	69 S		Fethard & Killusty 1806		
68	Kilvemnon	83 S	1805	Mullinahone 1809		
69	Knockgraffon	64 S		New Inn 1798		
70	Lattin	26 S		Lattin & Cullen 1846		
71	Lickfinn	76 S		Killenaule 1742		
72	Lismalin	80 S		Ballingarry 1814		
73	Lisronagh	104 S		Powerstown 1808		
74	Magorban	44 S		Killenaule 1742		
75	Magowry	47 S		Killenaule 1742		
76	Modeshil	81 S		Mullinahone 1809		
77	Molough	99 S		Newcastle 1814		
78	Mora	65 S		Powerstown 1808		
79	Mortlestown	86 S		Cahir 1776		
80	Mowney	79 S		Ballingarry 1814		
81	Neddans	98 S		Ardfinnan 1809		
82	Newcastle	100 S		Newcastle 1814		
83	Newchapel	103 S		Clerihan 1852		
84	Newtownlennan	113 S		Carrick-on-Suir 1784		
85	Oughterleague	8 S		Knockavilla 1834		
86	Outeragh	70 S		Cahir 1776		
87	Peppardstown	53 S		Drangan 1811		

NGA No.	CIVIL PARISH	GV No.	CHURCH OF IRELAND	ROMAN CATHOLIC	PRESBYTERIAN	OTHERS
88	Railstown	50 S		Fethard & Killusty 1806		
89	Rathcool	52 S		Killenaule 1742		
90	Rathkennan	1A S		Clonoulty 1804		
91	Rathlynin	13 S		Knockavilla 1834		
92	Rathronan	108 S		Powerstown 1808		
93	Redcity	61 S		Fethard & Killusty 1806		
94	Relickmurry & Athassel	21 S	1808	Golden 1833		
95	Rochestown	93 S		Ardfinnan 1809		
96	St. Johnbaptist	42 S	(Cashel Cathedral) 1668 Liberties of Cashel 1654 marriages	Cashel 1793 Killenaule 1742		Q. Cashel
97	St. Johnstown	46 S		Killenaule 1742		
98	St. Mary's Clonmel	114 S	1766	St. Mary's, Clonmel 1790 Powerstown 1808	Clonmel	B. Clonmel Q. Clonmel
99	St. Patricksrock	40 S		Cashel 1793		
100	Shanrahan	88 S	1793	Clogheen 1778		
101	Shronell	24 S		Lattin & Cullen 1846		
102	Solloghodbeg	11 S		Oola & Solohead 1809		
103	Solloghodmore	10 S		Oola & Solohead 1809		
104	Templebredon	15 S		Pallasgreen 1811		
105	Temple-etney	105 S		Kilsheelan 1840		
106	Templemichael	85 S	1791	Ballyneale 1839		
107	Templeneiry	34 S		Bansha & Kilmoyler 1820		
108	Templenoe	19 S		Tipperary 1793		

NGA No.	CIVIL PARISH	GV No.	CHURCH OF IRELAND	ROMAN CATHOLIC	PRESBYTERIAN	OTHERS
109	Templetenny	87 S		Ballyporeen 1817		
110	Tipperary	18 S	1779	Tipperary 1793	Tipperary	Q. Tipperary
111	Tubbrid	89 S		Ballylooby 1828		
112	Tullaghmelan	95 S	1823	Ardfinnan 1809		
113	Tullaghorton	96 S		Ballylooby 1828		
114	Tullamain	58 S		Cashel 1793 Fethard & Killusty 1806		
115	Whitechurch	90 S		Ballylooby 1828		

NGA No.	CIVIL PARISH	GV No.	CHURCH OF IRELAND	ROMAN CATHOLIC	PRESBYTERIAN	OTHERS
1	Aghaloo	38	or Caledon 1791 Brantry 1844	Aghaloo 1832	Caledon 1870 Ballymagrane 1851 Minterburn 1829	M. Caledon 1815 B. Crill
2	Aghalurcher	43	1787 Kiltermon 1861	Aghalurcher (Lisnaskea) 1835		
3	Arboe	27	1773	Arboe 1827		
4	Ardstraw	6	1847	Ardstraw East 1860 Ardstraw West 1843	Newtownstewart- 1st & 2nd 1848 (united 1903) Douglas 1831 1st Ardstraw 1831 2nd Ardstraw or Drumlegagh 1864	M. Newtown- stewart 1826
5	Artrea	22	1811	Artrea 1830	Moneymore 1827 Saltersland 1847	
6	Ballinderry	24	1802	Ballinderry 1826		
7	Ballyclog	26	1818	Ballyclog 1822	Albany (Stewartstown) 1838 Brigh 1836	
8	Bodoney Lower	8	1812	Bodoney Lower 1865	Gortin 1843 Badoney Crockatanty	
9	Bodoney Upper	7		Bodoney Upper 1866	Corrick or 2nd Donemana Glenelly	
10	Camus	5	1803	Camus 1773 Mourne 1866	Strabane - 1st 1828 2nd 1844	R.P. Strabane M. Strabane 1867
11	Cappagh	9	1753 Lislimnaghan 1862 Edenderry 1841	Cappagh 1843	Edenderry 1845 Crossroads or Mountjoy	M. Mayne 1831 B. Mullaghmore
12	Carnteel	37	1805	Aghaloo 1832	Aughnacloy 1812	M. Aughnacloy 1823
13	Clogher	40	1763 Fivemiletown 1804 Errigle Port- clare 1845 Augher 1866	Clogher 1825 Fivemiletown 1870	Clogher 1819 Aughentain 1836 Glenhoy 1850 Cavanaleck (Fivemiletown) 1836	M. Fivemiletown 1879
14	Clogherny	15	1859	Ballintacker (Beragh) 1832	Clogherny 1865 Seskinore or Newtonparry 1863	M. Beragh 1831 B. Seskinore
15	Clonfeacle	35		Clonfeacle 1814	Moy 1815 Benburb 1845 Eglish 1856	M. Moy 1874 B. Mullycar Q. Grange
16	Clonoe	31	1824	Clonoe 1806		

NGA No.	CIVIL PARISH	GV No.	CHURCH OF IRELAND	ROMAN CATHOLIC	PRESBYTERIAN	OTHERS
17	Derryloran	21	1796	Derryloran 1827	Sandholes 1844 Cookstown – 1st 1836 2nd & 3rd (united 1929)	M. Cookstown 1873 B. Cookstown
18	Desertcreat	25	1812	Desertcreight 1827		R.P. Grange
19	Donacavey	39	1777	Donaghcavey 1857	Ballynahatty – 1st & 2nd or Creevan 1843 (united 1928) Fintona 1836	M. Fintona 1878 B. Blackforth
20	Donaghedy	1	1697	Donaghedy or Dunamanagh 1854	Donaghedy – 1st & 2nd 1838 (united 1933) 1st Donemana	R.P. Bready
21	Donaghenry	28	1734 Brackaville 1836	Donaghenry 1822 Coalisland 1861	Stewartstown – 1st 1814 2nd (dissolved 1881) Newmills 1850	M. Newtownkelly 1830 M. Stewartstown 1868 C. Donaghy 1861
22	Donaghmore	32	1748	Donaghmore 1816	Castlecaulfield 1855 Clonaneese Upper 1868 Clonaneese Lower 1811	M. Castlecaul- field 1830
23	Dromore	16		Dromore 1833	Dromore 1835	
24	Drumglass	33	1665	Drumglass, Killyman & Tullyniskin 1821	Dungannon – 1st 1790 2nd (united 1928) Carland 1759	M. Dungannon 1830 B. Dungannon
25	Drumragh	13	1800 Clanabogan 1863	Drumragh 1846	Omagh – 1st 1845 2nd or Trinity 1821 Gillygooley 1848	M. Omagh B. Omagh
26	Errigal Keerogue	41	1812	Errigal Kieran 1847	Ballygawley 1842 Ballyreagh 1843	B. Ballygawley B. Knockconny
27	Errigal Trough	42	1809	Errigal Trough 1835		
28	Kildress	20	1794	Kildress 1835	Orritor 1831 Claggan 1848	M. Tullyroan 1874
29	Killeeshill	36		Killeeshil 1816		
30	Killyman	34	1741	Drumglass, Killyman & Tullyniskin 1821		M. Kinnego 1874 M. Labey 1830
31	Kilskeery	17	1767	Kilskerry 1840		

NGA No.	CIVIL PARISH	GV No.	CHURCH OF IRELAND	ROMAN CATHOLIC	PRESBYTERIAN	OTHERS
32	Learmount	3	1832	Learmount & Cumber Upper 1863		
33	Leckpatrick	2		Leckpatrick 1863	Leckpatrick 1838	
34	Lissan	19	1753	Lissan 1839		
35	Longfield East	12		Langfield 1846	Drumquin 1845	M. Drumquin 1831
36	Longfield West	11		Langfield 1846		
37	Magheracross	18		Kilskerry 1840		
38	Pomeroy	29		Pomeroy 1837	Pomeroy 1841	
39	Tamlaght	23	1801	Arboe 1827 Coagh 1865	Coagh 1839	
40	Termonamonagan	10	1812	Termonamonagan 1863	Killeter 1839	M. Aghyaran 1826
41	Termonmaguirk	14	Cooley or Sixmilecross 1836	Termonmaguirk 1834	Sixmilecross	
42	Tullyniskan	30	1794	Drumglass, Killyman & Tullyniskan 1821		
43	Urney	4	1813 Derg 1807 Sion Mills 1853	Urney	Urney 1837 Castlederg – 1st 1823 2nd 1880 Clady Sion Mills 1866	M. Castlederg 1826

NGA No.	CIVIL PARISH	GV No.	CHURCH OF IRELAND	ROMAN CATHOLIC	PRESBYTERIAN	OTHERS
1	Affane	19		Modelligo 1846		
2	Aglish	68	Villiertown 1821	Aglish 1837		
3	Ardmore	69		Ardmore 1823 Aglish 1837 Clashmore 1810 Dungarvan 1787 Ring 1813		
4	Ballygunner	58		St. John's 1759		
5	Ballylaneen	34		Stradbally 1805		
6	Ballymacart	74		Ardmore 1823 Ring 1813		
7	Ballynakill	51		St. John's 1759		
8	Clashmore	71		Clashmore 1810		
9	Clonagam	11	1741	Portlaw 1805		
10	Clonea	32		Abbeyside 1828		
11	Colligan	27		Kilgobnet 1848		
12	Corbally	66		Tramore 1786		
13	Crooke	60		Killea 1780		
14	Drumcannon	47		Tramore 1786		
15	Dungarvan	30	1741	Dungarvan 1787 Abbeyside 1828 Aglish 1837		
16	Dunhill	44		Dunhill 1829		
17	Dysert	6		Carrickbeg 1807		
18	Faithlegg	53		Killea 1780		
19	Fenoagh	8		Carrickbeg 1807		
20	Fews	25		Kilrossanty 1822		
21	Grange or Lisgenan	73		Ardmore 1823		
22	Guilcagn	12		Portlaw 1805		
23	Inishlounaught	1	1801	St. Mary's, Clonmel 1790		
24	Islandikane	48		Dunhill 1829 Tramore 1786		
25	Kilbarry	54		Tramore 1786 Trinity Without or Ballybricken 1797		
26	Kilbarrymeaden	36		Kill 1797		

COUNTY WATERFORD

NGA No.	CIVIL PARISH	GV No.	CHURCH OF IRELAND	ROMAN CATHOLIC	PRESBYTERIAN	OTHERS
27	Kilbride	46		Dunhill 1829		
28	Kilburne	42		Tramore 1786 Trinity Without or Ballybricken 1797		
29	Kilcaragh	57		St. John's 1759		
30	Kilcockan	17		Knockanore 1816		
31	Kilcop	59		Killea 1780		
32	Kilgobnet	23		Kilgobnet 1848 Abbeyside 1828		
33	Killaloan	4		Kilsheelan 1840		
34	Killea	65	1816	Killea 1780		
35	Killoteran	38	1769	Trinity Without or Ballybricken 1797		
36	Kill St. Lawrence	55		St. John's 1759		
37	Kill St. Nicholas	52	1730	Killea 1780		
38	Killure	56		St. John's 1759		
39	Kilmacleague	62		Tramore 1786		
40	Kilmacomb	63		Killea 1780		
41	Kilmeaden	37	1683	Portlaw 1805 Trinity Without or Ballybricken 1797		
42	Kilmolash	28		Aglish 1837 Modelligo 1846		
43	Kilmoleran	7		Carrickbeg 1807		
44	Kilronan	2, 43		Newcastle 1814 Tramore 1786		
45	Kilrossanty	24	1838	Kilrossanty 1822 Kilgobnet 1848		
46	Kilrush	31		Dungarvan 1787		
47	Kilsheelan	5		Kilsheelan 1840		
48	Kilwatermoy	16	1860 Tallow & Kilwatermoy 1772	Knockanore 1816		
48	Kinsalebeg	72	1848 marriages	Ardmore 1823 Clashmore 1810 Ring 1813		
50	Leitrim	13A		Kilworth 1829		
51	Lickoran	21		Touraneena 1851		

120

COUNTY WATERFORD

NGA No.	CIVIL PARISH	GV No.	CHURCH OF IRELAND	ROMAN CATHOLIC	PRESBYTERIAN	OTHERS
52	Lismore & Mocollop	14	1693 Cappoquin 1844	Lismore 1820 Cappoquin 1807 Ballyduff 1849	Lismore	
53	Lisnakill	41		Trinity Without or Ballybricken 1797		
54	Modelligo	20		Modelligo 1846 Touraneena 1851		
55	Monamintra	61		Tramore 1786		
56	Monksland	35	1836	Kill 1797		
57	Mothel	10		Clonea 1831		
58	Newcastle	40		Portlaw 1805		
59	Rathgormuck	9		Clonea 1831 Touraneena 1851		
60	Rathmoylan	67		Tramore 1786		
61	Reisk	45		Dunhill 1829		
62	Ringagonagh	70		Ring 1813		
63	Rossduff	64		Killea 1780		
64	Rossmire	26	1834	Kill 1797		
65	St. Mary's Clonmel	3	1766	St. Peter's & Paul's 1836	Clonmel	
66	Seskinan	22		Touraneena 1851		
67	Stradbally	33	1798	Stradbally 1805		
68	Tallow	15	& Kilwatermoy 1772	Tallow 1797 Lismore 1820		
69	Templemichael	18	1821	Knockanore 1816		
70	Waterford City					
a	St. John's Within	49		St. John's 1759		
b	St. John's Without	50		St. John's 1759		
c	St. Michael's	49		St. Patrick's 1731		
d	St. Olave's	49	Trinity & St. Olave's 1658	Trinity Within (Cathedral Parish) 1729		
e	St. Patrick's	49	1723	St. Patrick's 1731		
f	St. Peter's	49		Trinity Within (Cathedral Parish) 1729		
g	St. Stephen's Within	49		St. Patrick's 1731		

NGA No.	CIVIL PARISH	GV No.	CHURCH OF IRELAND	ROMAN CATHOLIC	PRESBYTERIAN	OTHERS
h	St. Stephen's Without	49		St. John's 1759		
i	Trinity Within	49	Trinity & St. Olave's 1658	Trinity Within (Cathedral Parish 1729)	Waterford – 1st 1770 2nd 1847 (united 1864)	M. Waterford B. Waterford Q. Waterford
j	Trinity Without	39	Trinity & St. Olave's 1658	Trinity Without or Ballybricken 1797		
71	Whitechurch	29		Aglish 1837		

NGA No.	CIVIL PARISH	GV No.	CHURCH OF IRELAND	ROMAN CATHOLIC	PRESBYTERIAN	OTHERS
1	Ardnurcher or Horseleap	50		Clara 1821		
2	Ballyloughloe	46		Drumraney 1834		
3	Ballymore	36		Ballymore 1824		
4	Ballymorin	38		Milltown 1781		
5	Bunown	30		Drumraney 1834		
6	Carrick	59		Mullingar 1737 Rochfortbridge 1816		
7	Castlelost	63		Rochfortbridge 1816		
8	Castletown-kindalen	51		Castletown 1829		
9	Churchtown	40		Churchtown 1825		
10	Clonarney	24		Clonmellon 1757		
11	Clonfad	62		Rochfortbridge 1816		
12	Conry	39		Churchtown 1825		
13	Delvin	27	1817	Delvin 1785 Clonmellon 1757		
14	Drumraney	32		Drumraney 1834		
15	Durrow	54		Tullamore 1801		
16	Dysart	43		Churchtown 1825		
17	Enniscoffey	58		Rochfortbridge 1816		
18	Faughalstown	7		Turbotstown 1777		
19	Foyran	1		Castlepollard 1763		
20	Kilbeggan	52		Kilbeggan 1818		
21	Kilbixy	13	1843	Ballinacargy 1837		
22	Kilbride	60		Kilbride 1845		
23	Kilcleagh	47		Moate & Colry 1823 Lemanaghan & Ballynahowen 1821		B. Moate Q. Moate
24	Kilcumny	23	Drumcree 1816	Collinstown 1784		
25	Kilcumreragh	49		Tubber 1821		

NGA No.	CIVIL PARISH	GV No.	CHURCH OF IRELAND	ROMAN CATHOLIC	PRESBYTERIAN	OTHERS
26	Kilkenny West	31	Kilkenny 1783	Kilkenny West 1829		
27	Killagh	28		Delvin 1785		
28	Killare	37		Ballymore 1824		
29	Killua	25		Clonmellon 1757		
30	Killucan	44	1700	Killucan 1821 Kinnegad 1827	Killucan (united with Mullingar 1929)	
31	Killulagh	26		Delvin 1785		
32	Kilmacnevan	12		Milltown 1781		
33	Kilmanaghan	48		Tubber 1821		
34	Kilpatrick	8		Collinstown 1784		
35	Lackan	15		Multyfarnham 1824		
36	Leny	17		Multyfarnham 1824		
37	Lickbla	2		Castlepollard 1763		
38	Lynn	56		Mullingar 1737		
39	Mayne	3	1808	Turbotstown 1777		
40	Moylisker	57		Mullingar 1737		
41	Mullingar	42		Mullingar 1737	Mullingar	
42	Multyfarnham	16		Multyfarnham 1824		
43	Newtown	53		Castletown 1829		
44	Noughaval	29		Drumraney 1834		
45	Pass of Kilbride	61		Kilbride 1845 Rochfortbridge 1816		
46	Piercetown	33		Moyvore 1831		
47	Portloman	22		Mullingar 1737		
48	Portnashangan	19		Multyfarnham 1824		
49	Rahugh	55		Kilbeggan 1818		B. Rahugh
50	Rathaspick	11		Rathaspick & Russagh 1819		
51	Rathconnell	41		Mullingar 1737 Taghmon 1781		

COUNTY WESTMEATH

NGA No.	CIVIL PARISH	GV No.	CHURCH OF IRELAND	ROMAN CATHOLIC	PRESBYTERIAN	OTHERS
52	Rathconrath	34		Milltown 1781		
53	Rathgarve	4		Castlepollard 1763		
54	Russagh	10		Rathaspick & Russagh 1819		
55	St. Feighins	5	Collinstown 1838	Collinstown 1784		
56	St. Mary's	6		Collinstown 1784		
57	St. Mary's (Athlone)	45	1746 Willbrooke Church 1756	St. Mary's (Athlone) 1813	Athlone	B. Athlone Q. Athlone
58	Stonehall	18		Taghmon 1781		
59	Street	9		Streete 1820		
60	Taghmon	21		Taghmon 1781		
61	Templeoran	14		Ballinacargy 1837		
62	Templepatrick	35		Moyvore 1831	Moyvore (united with Mullingar 1915)	
63	Tyfarnham	20		Taghmon 1781		

NGA No.	CIVIL PARISH	GV No.	CHURCH OF IRELAND	ROMAN CATHOLIC	PRESBYTERIAN	OTHERS
1	Adamstown	50	1802	Adamstown 1807		
2	Ambrosetown	102		Bannow 1830 Rathangan 1803 Taghmon 1801		
3	Ardamine	30	1807	Ballygarrett 1828		
4	Ardcandrisk	71		Glynn 1817		
5	Ardcavan	85		Castlebridge 1832		
6	Ardcolm	86		Castlebridge 1832		
7	Artramon	84		Crossbeg 1856		
8	Ballingly	80		Bannow 1830		
9	Ballyanne	46		Cushinstown 1752		
10	Ballybrazil	89		Suttons 1824		
11	Ballybrennan	126		Tagoat 1853		
12	Ballycanew	24	1733	Ballyoughter 1810		
13	Ballycarney	6	1835	Bunclody 1834 Marshallstown 1854		
14	Ballyconnick	103		Rathangan 1803		
15	Ballyhoge	53		Bree 1837		
16	Ballyhuskard	58		Monageer 1838 Oulart 1837 Oylegate 1803		
17	Ballylannan	79		Clongeen 1847		
18	Ballymitty	81		Bannow 1830		
19	Ballymore	129		Moyglass & Ballymore 1840		
20	Ballynaslaney	64		Oylegate 1803		
21	Ballyvaldon	62		Blackwater 1815		
22	Ballyvaloo	68		Blackwater 1815		
23	Bannow	105		Bannow 1830		
24	Carn	138	1815 burials	Lady's Island 1737		
25	Carnagh	54		Cushinstown 1752		
26	Carnew	3		Kilrush 1841		

NGA No.	CIVIL PARISH	GV No.	CHURCH OF IRELAND	ROMAN CATHOLIC	PRESBYTERIAN	OTHERS
27	Carrick	78		Glynn 1817		
28	Castle-ellis	60		Blackwater 1815 Oulart 1837		
29	Chapel	44		Cloughbawn 1816		
30	Clone	11		Monageer 1838		
31	Clongeen	72		Clongeen 1847		
32	Clonleigh	42		Rathnure 1846		
33	Clonmines	97		Tintern 1827		
34	Clonmore	45	1827	Bree 1837 Davidstown 1805		
35	Coolstuff	76		Glynn 1817 Taghmon 1801		
36	Crosspatrick	13		Tomacork 1785		
37	Donaghmore	31	Glasscarrig 1807	Ballygarrett 1828		
38	Doonooney	51		Adamstown 1807 Taghmon 1801		
39	Drinagh	120		Piercestown 1811		
40	Duncormick	106		Rathangan 1803		
41	Edermine	63		Oylegate 1803		
42	Ferns	7	& Kilbride 1775	Ferns 1819		
43	Fethard	99		Templetown 1792		
44	Hook	100		Templetown 1792		
45	Horetown	74		Clongeen 1847 Taghmon 1801		
46	Inch	16, 73	1726	Kilenieran 1852 Clongeen 1847		
47	Ishartmon	133		Moyglass & Ballymore 1840		
48	Kerloge	117		Wexford 1671		
49	Kilbride	8	& Ferns 1775	Ferns 1819		
50	Kilbrideglynn	77		Glynn 1817		
51	Kilcavan	19, 101		Kilenieran 1852 Bannow 1830		

NGA No.	CIVIL PARISH	GV No.	CHURCH OF IRELAND	ROMAN CATHOLIC	PRESBYTERIAN	OTHERS
52	Kilcomb	4		Ferns 1819		
53	Kilcormick	25		Monageer 1838 Oulart 1837		
54	Kilcowan	107		Rathangan 1803		
55	Kilcowanmore	52		Bree 1837		
56	Kildavin	118		Piercestown 1811		
57	Kilgarvan	69		Adamstown 1807 Clongeen 1847 Taghmon 1801		
58	Kilgorman	17		Arklow 1809		
59	Killag	109		Rathangan 1803		
60	Killann	36	1771	Rathnure 1846		
61	Killegney	43	1800	Cloughbawn 1816		
62	Killenagh	29		Ballygarrett 1828		
63	Killesk	93	1788	Ramsgrange 1835 Suttons 1824		
64	Killiane	122		Piercestown 1811		
65	Killila	61		Blackwater 1815		
66	Killincooly	33		Litter 1788 Oulart 1837		
67	Killinick	125	1804	Moyglass & Ballymore 1840		
68	Killisk	59		Castlebridge 1832 Oulart 1837		
69	Killurin	70	1816	Glynn 1817		
70	Kilmacree	123		Piercestown 1811		
71	Kilmakilloge	21	Gorey 1801	Gorey 1845		
72	Kilmallock	65	1813	Crossbeg 1856		
73	Kilmannan	104		Rathangan 1803		
74	Kilmokea	92		Suttons 1824		
75	Kilmore	110		Kilmore 1752		
76	Kilmuckridge	34		Litter 1788		
77	Kilnahue	18	1817	Camolin 1853 Craanford 1871		
78	Kilnamanagh	32	1818	Oulart 1837		

NGA No.	CIVIL PARISH	GV No.	CHURCH OF IRELAND	ROMAN CATHOLIC	PRESBYTERIAN	OTHERS
79	Kilnenor	15		Gorey 1845		
80	Kilpatrick	83	1836 burials	Crossbeg 1856		
81	Kilpipe	14	1828	Tomacork 1785		Q. Ballynabarney
82	Kilrane	131		Tagoat 1853		
83	Kilrush	2		Kilrush 1841 Bunclody 1834		
84	Kilscanlan	55		Cushinstown 1752		
85	Kilscoran	130		Tagoat 1853		
86	Kiltennell	28	1806	Ballygarrett 1828		
87	Kiltrisk	27		Ballygarrett 1828		
88	Kilturk	111		Kilmore 1752		
89	Ladysisland	136		Lady's Island 1737		
90	Liskinfere	23	1802	Ballyoughter 1810		
91	Maudlintown	116		Wexford 1671		
92	Mayglass	124		Moyglass & Ballymore 1840		
93	Meelnagh	35		Blackwater 1815 Litter 1788 Oulart 1837		
94	Monamolin	26		Monamolin 1834 Litter 1788		
95	Monart	10		Ballindaggin 1871 Marshallstown 1854		
96	Moyacomb	1	or Clonegal 1792	Clonegal 1833		
97	Mulrankin	108	1786	Kilmore 1752		
98	Newbawn	49		Adamstown 1807		
99	Oldross	48		Cushinstown 1752 Suttons 1824		
100	Owenduff	91	1752	Tintern 1827		
101	Rathaspick	119	1844	Piercestown 1811		
102	Rathmacknee	121	1813 burials	Piercestown 1811		

COUNTY WEXFORD

NGA No.	CIVIL PARISH	GV No.	CHURCH OF IRELAND	ROMAN CATHOLIC	PRESBYTERIAN	OTHERS
103	Rathroe	95		Ramsgrange 1835		
104	Rossdroit	38	1802	Davidstown 1805		
105	Rosslare	128		Tagoat 1853		
106	Rossminoge	20		Camolin 1853 Craanford 1871		
107	St. Helen's	132		Tagoat 1853		
108	St. Iberius	135		Lady's Island 1737		
109	St. James & Dunbrody	94		Ramsgrange 1835 Suttons 1824	Duncannon 1858	
110	St. John's	40, 113		Davidstown 1805 Enniscorthy 1794 Wexford 1671		
111	St. Margaret's	87, 137		Castlebridge 1832 Lady's Island 1737		
112	St. Mary's (Enniscorthy)	12	1798	Enniscorthy 1794	Enniscorthy	
113	St. Mary's (New Ross)	47	1763	New Ross 1789		C. New Ross
114	St. Mary's (Newtownbarry)	5	1779	Bunclody 1834		M. Newtownbarry
115	St. Michael's	127		Tagoat 1853		
116	St. Mullin's	41		St. Mullin's 1796 Borris 1782		
117	St. Nicholas	66		Castlebridge 1832		
118	St. Peter's	115		Wexford 1671		
119	Skreen	67		Castlebridge 1832		
120	Tacumshin	134	1832	Lady's Island 1737		
121	Taghmon	75		Taghmon 1801		
122	Tellarought	90		Cushinstown 1752		
123	Templeludigan	37		Rathnure 1846		
124	Templescoby	39	Templescobin 1802	Davidstown 1805		

NGA No.	CIVIL PARISH	GV No.	CHURCH OF IRELAND	ROMAN CATHOLIC	PRESBYTERIAN	OTHERS
125	Templeshanbo	9	1815	Enniscorthy 1794 Ballindaggin 1871 Bunclody 1834		
126	Templeshannon	57		Enniscorthy 1794 Monageer 1838		
127	Templetown	98		Templetown 1792		
128	Tikillin	82		Crossbeg 1856		
129	Tintern	96		Tintern 1827		
130	Tomhaggard	112	1809	Kilmore 1752		
131	Toome	22	1770	Ballyoughter 1810		
132	Wexford City	114	1674	Wexford 1671	Wexford 1844 (united with Enniscorthy 1925)	M. Wexford C. Wexford Q. Wexford
a	St. Bridget's	114				
b	St. Doologe's	114				
c	St. Iberius	114				
d	St. Mary's	114				
e	St. Michael's of Feagh	114				
f	St. Patrick's	114				
g	St. Peter's	115				
h	St. Selskar's	114				
133	Whitechurch	88		Suttons 1824		
134	Whitechurchglynn	56		Glynn 1817 Taghmon 1801		Q. Lambstown

NGA No.	CIVIL PARISH	GV No.	CHURCH OF IRELAND	ROMAN CATHOLIC	PRESBYTERIAN	OTHERS
1	Aghowle	55		Clonmore 1813		
2	Ardoyne	54		Clonmore 1813		
3	Arklow	50		Arklow 1809		
4	Ballinacor	34		Rathdrum 1795		
5	Ballintemple	47	1823	Arklow 1809		
6	Ballykine	37	Ballinaclash 1839	Rathdrum 1795		
7	Ballynure	15	1807	Baltinglass 1807		
8	Baltinglass	20		Baltinglass 1807		Q. Baltinglass
9	Blessington	2	1695	Blessington 1852 Blackditches (Valleymount) 1810		
10	Boystown	4		Blackditches (Valleymount) 1810		
11	Bray	12	1666	Bray 1800	Bray 1836	
12	Burgage	3		Blessington 1852		
13	Calary	23		Bray 1800 Glendalough 1807 Kilquade 1826		
14	Carnew	59	1749 Shillelagh 1833	Tomacork 1785		
15	Castlemacadam	44	(Ovoca) 1720	Avoca 1778 Kilbride & Barnderrig 1858		
16	Crecrin	53		Clonmore 1813		
17	Crehelp	6		Dunlavin 1815		
18	Crosspatrick	57	& Kilcommon 1830	Tomacork 1785		
19	Delgany	13	1666	Bray 1800 Kilquade 1826		
20	Derrylossary	24		Glendalough 1807		
21	Donaghmore	19		Dunlavin 1815		
22	Donard	9		Dunlavin 1815		
23	Drumkay	41		Wicklow 1747		
24	Dunganstown	43	1783	Kilbride & Barnderrig 1858		
25	Dunlavin	8	1697	Dunlavin 1815		

NGA No.	CIVIL PARISH	GV No.	CHURCH OF IRELAND	ROMAN CATHOLIC	PRESBYTERIAN	OTHERS
26	Ennereilly	46		Avoca 1778		
27	Freynestown	16		Dunlavin 1815		
28	Glenealy	33	1825	Wicklow 1747		
29	Hacketstown	35		Hacketstown 1820		
30	Hollywood	7		Ballymore Eustace 1779		
31	Inch	51		Arklow 1809		
32	Kilbride	1, 48		Blessington 1852 Avoca 1778		
33	Kilcommon	32, 38	1814 & Crosspatrick 1830	Wicklow 1747 Tomacork 1785		
34	Kilcoole	27		Kilquade 1826		
35	Killahurler	49		Arklow 1809		
36	Killiskey	30	1818	Ashford 1864		
37	Kilmacanoge	11		Bray 1800		
38	Kilpipe	40	1828	Killaveny 1800		
39	Kilpoole	42	Wicklow 1655	Wicklow 1747		M. Wicklow Q. Wicklow
40	Kilranelagh	21		Rathvilly 1797		
41	Kiltegan	22		Hacketstown 1820		
42	Knockrath	25		Rathdrum 1795		
43	Liscolman	52		Clonmore 1813		
44	Moyacomb	58	or Clonegal 1792	Clonegal 1833		
45	Moyne	36		Hacketstown 1820		
46	Mullinacuff	56	1838	Clonmore 1813		
47	Newcastle Lower	29	Newcastle 1666	Kilquade 1826		
48	Newcastle Upper	28	Newcastle 1666	Kilquade 1826		
49	Powerscourt	10	1677	Enniskerry 1825		
50	Preban	39	1827	Tomacork 1785		
51	Rathbran	18	Stratford-on-Slaney 1812	Baltinglass 1807		
52	Rathdrum	26	1706	Rathdrum 1795		
53	Rathnew	31		Ashford 1864		
54	Rathsallagh	14		Dunlavin 1815		

COUNTY WICKLOW

NGA No.	CIVIL PARISH	GV No.	CHURCH OF IRELAND	ROMAN CATHOLIC	PRESBYTERIAN	OTHERS
55	Rathtoole	17		Baltinglass 1807		
56	Redcross	45		Avoca 1778 Kilbride & Barnderrig 1858		
57	Tober	5		Dunlavin 1815		

92-307